Praise for Remote

"A wonderful, wildly original, illuminating book about the perils of being a citizen in a celebrity culture."

—DAVID HALBERSTAM

"A brilliant mix of scrapbook, cultural criticism, autobiography, travelogue, and found poetry.... Shields holds a mirror to society and sees himself. He holds a mirror to himself and sees society. And it is always a fun-house mirror—warped by irony and goofy insight. There are sections of this amazing, funny little book composed (beautifully) of nothing more than bumper-sticker slogans; there are pages of bold pronouncements, many of which are lacerating in their acuity."

—STEVEN REA, *Philadelphia Inquirer*

"A colorful gallery of cultural significance ... a lively and inventive collection of fifty-two short takes on contemporary American life.... What Shields reveals about himself and others is often wise, frequently hilarious, but not always comforting to hear. His deadpan wisecracks hang precipitously over despair—like a cross between Fran Lebowitz and Milan Kundera."

—JOHN HAWLEY, *San Francisco Chronicle*

"A witty and original cultural scribe and voice of his generation."

—IRENE LACHER, *Los Angeles Times*

"David Shields's *Remote*, a smart and disturbing collection of fifty-two short essays, dissects our obsession with image and television celebrity and, in the process, dissects the author himself.... Shields's book forces one to feel the insidious power of the desire to be connected to what everyone else is doing. He forces thought about the absurd little kinks in one's own responses to mass entertainment."

—THOMAS MALLON, *GQ*

"Breathtakingly intelligent ... electric insights ... cool, dry, arch irony ... addictive ..."

—LANCE OLSEN, *Review of Contemporary Fiction*

"What makes Shields's perspective on popular culture so interesting is its highly personal, even confessional nature: his essays often examine the private connections he feels to public figures and events.... Shields is a gifted writer capable of surprising perceptions and considerable wit, and his idiosyncratic book offers intriguing insights into the ways the media can shape both the identities and the perceptions of its viewers."

—*Publishers Weekly*

"I recently had a wonderful time reading *Remote*, by David Shields. It took me a day and a half of picking it up, putting it down, picking it up. I really love this book. I said to someone, 'You should read this book.' And she said, 'What's it about?' I said, 'I don't know exactly.' It's just an experience that you have with this object—this book—over the course of a couple of days."

—RAY SUAREZ, host, *Talk of the Nation*, NPR

"Frightening and funny and courageous. David Shields breaks every rule with perfect elegance. Then he tells the truth of an age."

—PAM HOUSTON

"One of 1996's slept-on gems, *Remote* is an extended, collage-style meditation on media, fame, distance, the nature of observation, and the location of one's self in all of these. As much reflexive autobiography broken into tiny chunks as pop cultural commentary, *Remote* is sharp, funny, poignant, and exceptionally media-savvy, featuring a David Shields who can pull apart complicated relationships between observer and observed with poetic ease."

—JOE GROSS, *Austin American-Statesman*

"The terrain of celebrity culture is constantly shifting ground, and what Shields has invented is, at least, a new way to map the landscape."

—BRAD TYER, *Houston Chronicle*

"By turns sardonic and tender, this really quite brilliant book crafts fragments of the cultural landscape into a telling commentary on the American obsession with confession, personality, celebrity, image, simulacrum."

—PETER BROOKS

"In a series of vivid verbal snapshots, David Shields's *Remote* captures an all too familiar America frighteningly obsessed with fame. Shields's postmodern memoir provides an ironic conduit to a media-mad society. In fifty-two short takes, Shields brilliantly takes the measure of America."

—JANICE LEE, *Elle*

"Shields's ruminations on life and culture are not just a diary of experience, a chronicle of his willing embrace of our culture. Rather, this strange little book ... achieves a kind of hypnotic power by Shields's standing apart from his subjects. He is a trenchant observer, a talent no doubt honed through learning to manage the stuttering that marked his childhood and youth (and that became the subject of his second novel, *Dead Languages*).... *Remote* is an iconoclastic and unclassifiable, quirky and irreverent meditation on the cluttered surface of late twentieth-century American life."

—DONN FRY, *Seattle Times*

"Unclassifiable, wayward, inspired, and very funny, *Remote* is one of the most intelligently self-exposing books I've encountered in a long time. By documenting his own sensibility without insisting that it be representative, David Shields strikes wild chords in this reader."

—WAYNE KOESTENBAUM

Remote

Also by David Shields

Enough About You: Adventures in Autobiography
"Baseball Is Just Baseball": The Understated Ichiro
Black Planet: Facing Race during an NBA Season
A Handbook for Drowning: Stories
Dead Languages: A Novel
Heroes: A Novel

Remote

*Reflections on Life in the
Shadow of Celebrity*

David Shields

with a foreword by Phillip Lopate

THE UNIVERSITY OF WISCONSIN PRESS

The University of Wisconsin Press
1930 Monroe Street
Madison, Wisconsin 53711

www.wisc.edu/wisconsinpress/

3 Henrietta Street
London WC2E 8LU, England

1   3   5   4   2

Printed in the United States of America

Library of Congress Cataloging-in-Publication Data

Shields, David.
Remote / David Shields ; foreword by Phillip Lopate.
p. c.m.
ISBN 0-299-19364-0 (pbk. : alk. paper)
1. Shields, David. 2. Authors, American—20th century—Biography. I. Title
PS3569.H4834 Z476   2004
813'54 B—dc21   2003006269

Grateful acknowledgment is made to the following for permission to
reprint previously published material: excerpt from *The World as Will and
Representation*, vol. 2, by Arthur Schopenhauer, translated by E. F. J. Payne
(New York: Dover Publications, 1966), reprinted by permission of Dover
Publications; excerpt from "Esthetique du Mal," from *The Collected Poems* by
Wallace Stevens, copyright © 1947 by Wallace Stevens, reprinted by permission
of Alfred A. Knopf, Inc.; excerpt from "Audiogenic Epilepsy Induced by a
Specific Television Performer," by Venkat Ramani, M.D. (*The New England
Journal of Medicine*, vol. 325, no. 2, July 11, 1991, pp. 134–135), reprinted by
permission of the *New England Journal of Medicine*; "Around Pastor
Bonhoeffer," from *Passing Through: The Later Poems New and Selected*
by Stanley Kunitz, copyright © 1970 by Stanley Kunitz, reprinted by
permission of W. W. Norton & Company, Inc. "The System," from *Three
Poems* by John Ashbery, copyright © 1970 by John Ashbery, reprinted by
permission of the Viking Press, Inc.

For Laurie

Acknowledgments

I'd like to thank the National Endowment for the Arts, PEN/Revson Foundation, Artist Trust, Centrum Foundation, Seattle Arts Commission, and King County Arts Commission for grants that enabled me to complete this book, and the following people for their assistance: Patricia Pierce Hutton, Deborah Norden, David Platzker, Robyn Ricks, Milton Shields, Paula Shields, Theresa Venice, and Michelle Werner. Special thanks to Vicki Demetre for her invaluable work as photo consultant.

Foreword

The recent memoir craze in publishing had not gone on long before it began to provoke a backlash and a crisis. The backlash, from various fastidious literary critics, expressed disgust at the narcissism of nobodies ("How dare these neophyte authors think we care about them and their problems?"), and a drawing of the skirts up from the muck of "untransformed" experience, as well as a certain commercial envy. Such principled or resentful disdain alone would not have been sufficient to provoke a crisis, but sales began to diminish, indicating that the public itself, having sampled the lives and traumas of several dozen representative strangers, was experiencing some satiety with the form. Of course, historically speaking, autobiographical writing is too established a literary practice ever to peak and ebb; but the "new memoir" has, for the moment at least, been put on the defensive. It needs some fresh thinking and formal innovation.

Along comes David Shields to take up the job. Refusing to cast his life in the pious scenarios of the recovery movement, with its convenient narrative arc of victimization, addiction, denial, revelation, and faith, he insists on trying to convey the unredeemed flotsam and jetsam of daily American experience. Rather than evading the charge of self-absorption with a show of false humility, or self-justifying claims of acute suffering leading to triumph, he dives right into the comedy of narcissism, unraveling its extraordinary pettiness and insecurity. The reader is free to identify (squeamishly, of course) or feel superior. But either way, you had better be aware that Shields knows full well what he is doing: a part of him wants naturally to be loved, another part wants to provoke and irritate. He shows courage and sophistication in playing at the borders of acceptance, as well as in interrogating the autobiographical tradition (note the references to Rousseau, Nabokov, Trow). In the end, *Remote* is not so much a memoir as a meditation on memoirs, on the pleasures and pitfalls of autobiographical writing.

Remote is both a book very much of its time and ahead of its time. It is clearly topical in focusing on America's fascination with celebrity, and the fear that one is not really alive unless the media had fastened on oneself. We are shown in these pages the humiliation that people will put themselves through to be used by the media. Beyond that, we are brought face to face with the underlying anxiety of identity.

What is the nature of the individual self in today's consumer culture? Are our thoughts even our own, or are we merely channeling messages from the mass media, which function as a kind of exoskeleton. Martin Buber wrote: "The perception of one's fellow man as a whole, as a unity, and as unique—even if his wholeness, unity, and uniqueness are only partly developed, as is usually the case—is opposed in our time by almost everything that is commonly understood as specifically modern." Shields scrupulously gives appropriate weight to the colonized self, brainwashed by tribal inputs, while at the same time insisting that yes, we are individuals, in the old, humanist sense of the term, if only by virtue of our petty spite, our unresolvable desires, and our inexplicable tenderness for the world's detritus.

Shields is a master of the fragment, which allows him to spotlight the isolated geekiness of a particular subject, while also weaving thematic links between the pieces. Each fragment can be a mini-essay, a prose poem, a list (see his brilliant catchment of clichés in "Always"), a vignette, or some other framing device. The white space between sections permits easy jumps from the personal to the impersonal, the trivial to the lofty. By employing this mosaic technique, Shields operates here in an essayistic line that includes Joan Didion and Richard Rodriguez, and which can be traced back to the seminal Walter Benjamin, with his "One Way Street" and "A Berlin Childhood" suites that collaged recollections with speculative analyses about modern forms of advertising and coping. In this modernist tradition, the fragment underscores the lack of coherence and causality in contemporary experience, and in the individual self.

One might also try to place Shields in the literary generation of such hyperventilating, hyper-footnoting, "voice" writers as David Foster Wallace, Rick Moody, Nicholson Baker, and Dave Eggers. All of these experimental stylists have camped out at the intersection between high and low culture, fiction and nonfiction, reliable witnessing and hypertrophied rationalization, or obsessive logorrhea. They reflect the postmodernist fascination with the undecidability of any one truth.

Shields, too, questions his reliability as a mature witness by worrying the perspectival flaw alluded to in the title: remoteness, remote control, detachment, an inability to engage with life, etc. He provides us with a set of alternate lenses, such as friends who criticize his character, or "almost famous" alter egos, such as David Milch, Bob Balaban, "Stuttering John" Melendez, and Joseph Schildkraut, who enact career trajectories that suggestively aggrandize or diminish his own sense of self. Having said all that, I would add that Shields's persona is more grounded, attractive, warm, cohesive and optimistic than his use of fragments and self-disclaimers would suggest. Overall, he comes off as a mensch.

In *Remote*, as in Shields's successive forays into autobiographical writing, *Black Planet* and *Enough About You*, we become extremely familiar with certain elements of the "I"-character: his stuttering, his liberal journalist parents, his Jewishness, his obsession with sports and movies, his awkward adolescence, his graduate school apprenticeship as a writer, his identification with Seattle, and so on. We also become privy to more minute details, preferences, habits, tics, of such particularity that you almost have to go back to the great Montaigne to find an equivalently miniscule self-scrutiny. He confides, for instance: "I prefer previews to the movie, the 'about the author' notes in the back of literary magazines to the contents of the magazine, the pregame hype to the game.... In social situations in which it would be to my disadvantage to appear heterosexual, I attempt to give the impression that it's not beyond my ken to be bisexual.... I'm drawn to affectless people whose emptiness is a kind of frozen pond on which I excitedly skate." Shields shares

with Montaigne the conviction that it is precisely these secret little
peculiarities, barely acknowledged by oneself, that make a person
discretely individual and human.

Along with Wayne Koestenbaum and Daniel Harris, Shields has
gone the farthest of his generation, I think, in taking risks with
autobiographical writing. He mocks naked self-absorption until
it turns into its obverse, the dissolution of the ego. That is why
I said earlier that this book might have been ahead of its time:
when *Remote* first appeared, in 1996, it was met with delight by the
cognoscenti, and incomprehension by the squares. Now we have a
second chance to savor what Shields has been up to.

PHILLIP LOPATE

You want to put in a little bit of David—the safe part of David—the David that you wouldn't be afraid to show to anybody, but there is a David that you don't want to be in the film, and that David may be the truth, and that's what you should try to put in the film if you don't dare face yourself other ways. Confess things to the camera. I don't know. Say the things that you're most ashamed of, things that you don't want to remember, things that you don't want anybody to know. Maybe that way there'll be some truth. Or perhaps you should take off all your clothes and stand in front of the camera for hours and not do anything. Just stand in front of the camera. Perhaps something magical will happen. Perhaps some truth will come out. I'm not sure.

—JIM MCBRIDE, *David Holzman's Diary*

Remote

Prologue
Life Story

This book isn't concerned with the psychodynamics of the American nuclear family. It's neither a coming-of-age novel nor a love story. It's a self-portrait given over to a single subject and splintered into fifty-two pieces. I'm reading my life as if it were an allegory, an allegory about remoteness, and finding evidence wherever I can.

All the time I think about how I want *Remote* to be such a big hit that I'm invited onto morning television shows to offer scintillating disquisitions upon *that very camera which is now pointed directly at me* . . .

"The attraction of inappropriate attention, aspiration, and affection to a *shimmer* spins out, in its operation, a little mist of energy which is rather like love, but trivial, rather like a sense of home, but apt to disappear. In this mist exists the Aesthetic of the Hit."[1]

"My parents didn't preach against these things themselves but against wanting these things," I hear a famous author say. "I didn't know how to get these things without wanting them."

"I'm no longer just a person," the famous author says on another occasion, feigning disgruntlement. "I'm a personality."

The Nimbus of Her Fame
Makes a Nullity of Us All

It seems to me that "real" people such as the inept athlete Bob Uecker or the overweight Oprah Winfrey—celebrities who were once unsuccessful or, in some other notable way, "flawed"—play a crucial role in keeping our hopes alive. In Oprah's transition from fat to thin, from poor to rich, we see the possibility of our own transformation. I think of all those comedians who live in Los Angeles but never stop talking about New York, as if to say, "I once was lost (existed in life) and now am found (exist only on TV)."

This afternoon's *Seattle Today* television program is devoted to Oprah's appearance, and I attend the taping. The KING-5 lobby features huge TV screens everywhere and couches like thrones. Everybody looks like they're going to church—dressed up, serious, whispery, slightly nervous. A plate of chocolate chip cookies with M&M's serve as a kind of metaphor for pre- and post-Oprah; either we are, in Oprah's phrase, "ordinary folk," or we belong on the outsized television screen on which, at three in the afternoon, preternaturally attractive soap-opera figures play. Between us and Oprah is this plate of cookies. I, too, want to be rich and thin and famous. I abstain.

Before the show, one woman says to another, "I think your hair looks great."

"A little bit too curly. But Carey has coiffed her hair for the event."

Another woman says, "I saw Oprah on *The Tonight Show*. When she was talking about her weight going up and down, she spoke right to me."

Someone else says, "Hi. I'm from the sexual harassment committee."

The set of the show is made up of magazines, pink couches, wood painted blue and pink, flowers, vases, books, plates, and paintings of nothing, absolutely nothing—pastels and vague landscapes. It isn't anyone's living room.

"I have a friend who looks like Candice Bergen," says a member of the press sitting next to me. "She lives in New York and everyone always mistakes her. It's so funny."

"No one looks that similar," says her colleague.

A KING-person asks if we're all big Oprah fans. Not fans of the big Oprah, but big fans, enthusiastic devotees of Oprah. Applause. A member of the audience informs us that she has sung "The Star-Spangled Banner" at the Kingdome and offers to entertain us while we wait for Oprah. The offer is noted. "This is your opportunity to talk to Oprah, so start thinking of things, okay?" asks another KING-person, in a manner remarkably similar to that of Miss Gordon, my first-grade teacher: all solicitous concern and benign neglect.

"I just wanted to make sure you guys know you won't be asking any questions during the show," the KING-publicist tells the press people.

"Oh, no, we're going to be *harassing* her," says the reporter whose friend looks like Candice Bergen. Everyone laughs; the runway has been cleared for takeoff.

"Who are we here for?" a KING-person asks the audience.

"*Oprah!*" we shout.

"One more time!"

"*Oprah!*"

"I know that with Oprah here, you won't need to be told to applaud. But when the APPLAUSE sign lights up, be able to applaud, okay?"

APPLAUSE sign.

Applause.
"Again."
APPLAUSE sign.
Applause.

The hosts of *Seattle Today,* Cliff Lenz and Susan Michaels, come out to prime the audience before Oprah actually appears. As the audience applauds, Susan makes the oddest noise, which I can equate only with the sound of a seal, as if, without meaning to, she's trying to produce for us—in parody form—the essential ingredient of our well-trained reaction. Cliff wonders why there are so many children in the audience on a school day. He's informed that it's a school holiday.

"Public schools, too?" he asks.

Cliff and Susan ask what sort of questions people will want to ask Oprah when she's on the show. People want to ask her what she'll do with her "fat clothes"; whether she's ever heard of the actress Dorothy Dandridge, who was the questioner's sister; what Oprah's most significant career break was. All of the questions have to do, in other words, with the gap between regular life and celebrity. Someone tells Cliff that she's going to ask Oprah whether she'll pose for a picture with her. Cliff explains that Oprah is awfully busy and may not have the time.

"Well, that's the thing," the woman says. "I don't want you to answer. I want her to answer."

What Susan wants to know is: "What does she wear when she's kicking around the house? I'll bet she's my kind of lady—a sweats kind of lady." Susan looks like she's never seen the inside of a sweatband in her life. Reality keeps getting praised, weirdly, in the middle of this discourse, whose every syllable is fantasy.

"Oprah's almost here," we're informed.

"She's in the dressing room."

"We like to tease," says a KING-person, stoking the crowd, pumping his fist à la Arsenio Hall (who was still on the air then).

"Suck it in, folks," says Cliff. "You look fatter on the air."

"The things that bring me pleasure are the things that bring other people pleasure," Oprah tells us.

"What brings you happiness?"

"A great book."

Later, asked to name her two favorite books, she names two books she's attempting to develop into movies.

"What have you learned from guests, great or not?" she's asked.

She's learned the most from "ordinary folks, just an ordinary family. I believe we're all ordinary people."

Someone from the Rape Crisis Center wants to know whether Oprah's ever going to do a show on male victims of rape. Someone from the Northwest Women's Law Center wants to know what she thinks about abortion, then gives her a packet and a note from Gloria Steinem. "From Gloria?" Oprah asks. Someone from a volunteer organization asks if she's going to do a show about "volunteers, the ordinary heroes of this country."

Oprah failed as a television reporter because she'd always get all choked up on the air about the people whose tragedies she was relating. As an actress, she always cries over everyone else's scenes; when it comes time for her to cry, she's all dried up. In other words, she can't help it: she's just too empathetic.

"Has anyone on your show ever been rude, snobby, or arrogant?"

"No."

"Never?"

"No. Never."

When asked what her message is, she says she hopes that people will see the light in her and think there's maybe a little bit of that, too, in themselves.

"I hate to break," says Cliff, "but this is TV."

"Didn't she do a great job?" we're asked at the end of the show, and told to applaud one last time as she walks off the stage, leaving behind the packet the woman from the Northwest Women's Law

Center had given her. *The Oprah Winfrey Show* is being broadcast on the huge screen in the lobby as we exit. The topic is stand-up comedians.

When I get home, I find a message from the KING-publicist on my answering machine. I'd forgotten to wait around to find out whether a ticket for Oprah's Saturday night performance at the Paramount will be left for me at the Four Seasons Hotel, where Oprah's staying. "I hope there wasn't a problem and that's why you left," says the publicist—precursor of a new race of people who love problems and solutions to problems.

Problems and Solutions to Problems

We're all immersed in the cure-culture, though, or at least I am. I go to the state capitol in Olympia to receive a "Governor's Writers Award" for a book I wrote. A dozen other writers also receive awards, and they all give the standard acceptance speeches. I have the usual speech written out, too, but listening to everyone, I suddenly want to say something a little different, and the only thing I can think of concerns the autobiographical origins of the book, so I quickly write out a different speech:

> My novel *Dead Languages* began many years ago when I was simultaneously a graduate student in creative writing at the University of Iowa Writers' Workshop and a patient in the University of Iowa speech and hearing clinic. I was struck by the irony that as a writer I could control language but that as a stutterer I was to a certain extent at the mercy of it. *Dead Languages* explores language as a difficulty and a burden but also as human definition, as saving grace.

The audience responds warmly, but I feel more than a little cheap afterward, as if the only way I have to distinguish myself isn't through the work itself but through phrasing my life as a victim/victory narrative.

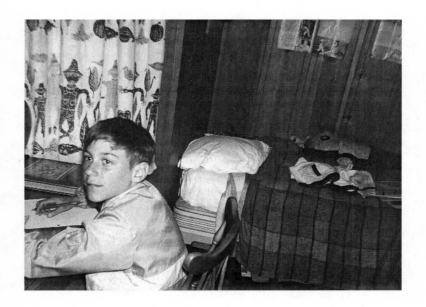

Information Sickness

Another such narrative goes like this: I love all forms of taxonomy—lists, categories, compartments, containers, boundaries. When I went to the famous Amsterdam sex shops, I was struck mainly by the arrangement of movies and magazines into exceedingly minute subdivisions of pleasure and pain. I love doing errands, and what I especially love about doing errands is crossing things off my errand list. When making phone calls, running errands, or performing ablutions, I always begin with what seems to me the least personal item and conclude with what seems to me the most personal item.

I much prefer this new system whereby a computerized voice rather than the operator gives you the number you want. The sound of long-distance interference on the phone or static on the car radio is, to me, reassuring, sensuous, even beautiful. I'm happy to play phone tag for weeks on end in order to avoid actually talking, let alone meeting, with someone. And yet if I walk past a ringing pay phone, I answer it; if I walk past a pay phone that's off the hook, I put the phone back on the receiver. I sometimes get so convinced that an answer I'm looking for—the answer to what I never know—can be found somewhere in the phone book that I'll spend the better portion of the afternoon flipping through the Yellow Pages.

The moment I walk in the door I check my snail mail, voice mail, e-mail, and fax machine, then turn on the TV, which I turn off when I go to sleep. The worst drunk I know—twelve-ounce tumblers of scotch at eight in the morning—leaves CNN on all night downstairs as a sort of lifeline in his sleep. (He's always talking about "black": black air is considered the ultimate sin; he can't tolerate black; "they went to black"; the famous six minutes of black—he's obsessed with black, afraid of it, secretly thrilled by its suggestion of depth.) I don't ordinarily drink coffee, but once, in order to stay up all night, I drank twelve cups in eight hours; the next morning, I walked into a Chec Medical Center and said, "Please, you've got to do something to turn my brain off." When I'm nervous and need to calm down, I chew blank three-by-five cards like a woodchuck.

I once ate a half-gallon carton of ice cream in a single sitting. Ditto a bag of sixty-four cookies. I know no purer joy than residence in the throes of sugar shock: the exact moment, just before you crash, when your brain turns off and you leave the planet. Before seeing friends I haven't seen for a long time, I go on a diet because I want people to think *he doesn't seem to seek solace in overeating; he must be happy and focused.*

Upon finding misplaced possessions I get almost weepily ecstatic. Once, immediately after the breakup of a relationship, I managed to lose my wallet, checkbook, and address book within the space of a week. I find that if I'm having trouble remembering something— the name of a movie, say, or a friend's phone number—I often inadvertently trigger memory by holding the item (such as a video guide or my address book) housing the information.

I prefer previews to the movie, the "about the author" notes in the back of literary magazines to the contents of the magazine, pregame hype to the game. I strongly prefer reading newspapers or magazines I purchase at the newsstand to newspapers or magazines I subscribe to. If I'm reading a book and it seems truly interesting, I tend to start reading back to front in order not to be too deeply under the sway of forward progress.

Once, a movie marquee's misspelling of the word "nominations" irritated me so much that when the punkette in the booth outside expressed zero interest in my correction, I bought a ticket for the movie, which I'd already seen, in order to be able to go inside and urge someone to do something about the error.[2] On the other hand, in sixth grade I "liked" a girl named Connie Cummings; classmates wrote in chalk on the playground, "DS + CC = Dog Shit + Cow Crap," which, to their surprise and perhaps Connie's as well, didn't bother me in the least: it seemed, simply, clever.

I've never seen my mother, whose maiden name was Hannah Bloom, happier than when she noticed that the *New York Times* crossword puzzle clue for 5-across was "Hard-hearted girl" and the clue for 7-across was "Claire of films." But my parents hoped so strongly that my sister and I would never "become part of the system" that they were honestly chagrined when, at age fifteen, I received my Social Security number, whereas my main response when I recently got audited by the IRS or saw my TRW credit report was a kind of relief that my existence could be confirmed by outside sources.

When I'm intending to jog and being watched, I pick up my pace and really run, but when no longer being watched, I go back to jogging. In conversation I feel little compunction about asking people extremely intimate questions but tend to balk when asked even the most moderately personal question myself. In social situations in which it would be to my disadvantage to appear heterosexual, I attempt to give the impression that it's not beyond my ken to be bisexual. At a Halloween party a few years ago, costumed as a pirate, I was flirting with a woman dressed as a lioness until she told me to take off my sunglasses, then said, "Oh, you're Jewish!"; my eyes were Jewish.

If a new song grabs my heart, I'll typically play it over and over again until it's completely robbed of all significance, beauty, and power. At a museum bookstore I bought dozens of postcards, none of which had any human figures on them, and the cashier said, "You know, you might be saying something here about yourself." I was: I'm drawn to affectless people whose emptiness is a kind of frozen pond on which I excitedly skate.

I have a persistent yearning that I don't have to live, exactly, anywhere. When I lived for a few years in New York, I'd go out every night at eleven and come back with the next day's *Times* and a pint of ice cream, then eat the whole carton while reading the paper, which had the odd but, I suppose, desired effect of blotting out tomorrow before it had even happened. All my nightmares—an endless network of honeycombs, a thousand cracks in a desiccated lake, a set of rotten teeth—are specifically about uncontrolled proliferation. Two questions constantly occur to me: what would this look like filmed? what would the soundtrack be? I grew up at a very busy intersection, and to me aesthetic bliss was hearing the sound of brakes screeching, then waiting for the sound of the crash.

I've read every bumper sticker I've ever seen.

Life Story

First things first.

You're only young once, but you can be immature forever. I may grow old, but I'll never grow up. Too fast to love, too young to die. Life's a beach.

Not all men are fools—some are single. 100% Single. I'm not playing hard to get—I am hard to get. I love being exactly who I am.

Heaven doesn't want me and Hell's afraid I'll take over. I'm the person your mother warned you about. Ex-girlfriend in trunk. Don't laugh—your girlfriend might be in here.

Girls wanted, all positions, will train. Playgirl on board. Party girl on board. Sexy blonde on board. Not all dumbs are blonde. Never underestimate the power of redheads. Yes, I am a movie star. 2QT4U. A4NQT. No ugly chicks. No fat chicks. I may be fat, but you're ugly and I can diet. Nobody is ugly after 2 A.M.

Party on board. Mass confusion on board. I brake for bong water. Jerk off and smoke up. Elvis died for your sins. Screw guilt. I'm Elvis—kiss me.

Ten and a half inches on board. Built to last. You can't take it with you, but I'll let you hold it for a while.

Be kind to animals—kiss a rugby player. Ballroom dancers do it with rhythm. Railroaders love to couple up. Roofers are always on top. Pilots slip it in.

Love sucks and then you die. Gravity's a lie—life sucks. Life's a bitch—you marry one, then you die. Life's a bitch and so am I. Beyond bitch.

Down on your knees, bitch. Sex is only dirty when you do it right. Liquor up front—poker in the rear. Smile—it's the second-best thing you can do with your lips. I haven't had sex for so long

I forget who gets tied up. I'm looking for love but will settle for sex. Bad boys have bad toys. Sticks and stones may break my bones, but whips and chains excite me. Live fast—love hard—die with your mask on.

So many men, so little time. Expensive but worth it. If you're rich, I'm single. Richer is better. Shopaholic on board. Born to shop. I'd rather be shopping at Nordstrom. Born to be pampered. A woman's place is the mall. When the going gets tough, the tough go shopping. Consume and die. He who dies with the most toys wins. She who dies with the most jewels wins. Die, yuppie scum.

This vehicle not purchased with drug money. Hugs are better than drugs.

You are loved.

Expectant mother on board. Baby on board. Family on board. I love my kids. Precious cargo on board. Are we having fun yet? Baby on fire. No child in car. Grandchild in back.

I fight poverty—I work. I owe, I owe, it's off to work I go. It sure makes the day long when you get to work on time. Money talks—mine only knows how to say goodbye. What do you mean I can't pay off my Visa with my MasterCard?

How's my driving? Call 1-800-545-8601. If this vehicle is being driven recklessly, please call 1-800-EAT-SHIT. Don't drink and drive—you might hit a bump and spill your drink.

My other car is a horse. Thoroughbreds always get there first. Horse lovers are stable people. My other car is a boat. My other car is a Rolls-Royce. My Mercedes is in the shop today. Unemployed? Hungry? Eat your foreign car. My other car is a 747. My ex-wife's car is a broom. I think my car has PMS. My other car is a piece of shit, too. Do not wash—this car is undergoing a scientific dirt test. Don't laugh—it's paid for. If this car were a horse, I'd have to shoot it. If I go any faster, I'll burn out my hamsters. I may be slow, but I'm ahead of you. I also drive a Titleist. Pedal downhill.

Shit happens. I love your wife. Megashit happens. I'm single again. Wife and dog missing—reward for dog. The more people I meet, the more I like my cat. Nobody on board. Sober 'n' crazy. Do it sober. Drive smart—drive sober.

No more Mr. Nice Guy. Lost your cat? Try looking under my tires. I love my German shepherd. Never mind the dog—beware

of owner. Nuke the gay whales. Don't fence me in. Don't tell me
what kind of day to have. Don't tailgate or I'll flush. Eat shit and
die. My kid beat up your honor student. Abort your inner child. I
don't care who you are, what you're driving, who's on board, who
you love, where you'd rather be, or what you'd rather be doing.

Not so close—I hardly know you. Watch my rear end, not hers.
You hit it—you buy it. Hands off. No radio. No Condo/No MBA/
No BMW. You toucha my car—I breaka your face. Protected by
Smith & Wesson. Warning: This car is protected by a large sheet of
cardboard.

LUV2HNT. Gun control is being able to hit your target.
Hunters make better lovers: they go deeper into the bush—they
shoot more often—and they eat what they shoot.

Yes, as a matter of fact, I do own the whole damn road. Get in,
sit down, shut up, and hold on. I don't drive fast—I just fly low. If
you don't like the way I drive, stay off the sidewalk. I'm polluting
the atmosphere. Can't do 55.

I may be growing old, but I refuse to grow up. Get even: Live
long enough to become a problem to your kids. We're out spending our children's inheritance.

Life is pretty dry without a boat. I'd rather be sailing. A man's
place is on his boat. Everyone must believe in something—I believe
I'll go canoeing. Who cares!

Eat dessert first—life is uncertain. Why be normal?

Don't follow me—I'm lost, too. Wherever you are, be there. No
matter where you go, there you are. Bloom where you are planted.

Easy does it. Keep it simple, stupid. I'm 4 Clean Air. Go fly a
kite. No matter—never mind. UFOs are real. Of all the things I've
lost, I miss my mind the most. I brake for unicorns.

Choose death.

Life Story

Choosing life, how do I write about it? The contrast between the title of Vladimir Nabokov's autobiography and the title of his first English-language novel suggests what is, for me, the difference between autobiography and fiction. *Speak, Memory: An Autobiography Revisited* is an extremely self-conscious name for a book. "Speak, Memory" is a mock classical address from the author to his own memory; "An Autobiography Revisited" is Nabokov's arch way of saying that the present volume is the revised edition of *Conclusive Evidence.* Into one phrase Nabokov has compressed the central motif of his memoir: autobiography is a physical place to which one can return, and memory can talk—consciousness is king. *The Real Life of Sebastian Knight* is an equally loaded title, for "real life" implies that lived life, rather than remembered or imagined life, is real; that here (we think) we're going to get the goods on a writer's real life, as if the life of an artist were to be found anywhere except in his work. In a book about half-brothers, "Sebastian" can be taken as a reference to Viola's twin brother in *Twelfth Night,* and Nabokov makes certain we know that "Knight" puns on "night," "chess knight," and "dubbed knight."

Note the differences: we interpret both titles, but the novel title makes references to the world as well as to literature, whereas the autobiography title is aggressively hermetic. Furthermore, the novel title assumes a sophistication beyond us and therefore an implicit antagonism toward us, for certainly readers who approach *The Real Life of Sebastian Knight* with the expectation that they're going to get the "real life" of Sebastian Knight are deceived. The autobiography title, on the other hand, takes the reader into its confidence; explains the entire ensuing book in its five-words-and-a-colon;

acknowledges and reveals, via its use of the imperative, the yearning of its own voice, the terror and ecstasy of its own creation, the
rapid heart ("some forty-five hundred heartbeats an hour") of its
creator.[3]

Radio

Autobiography, then. When I was in sixth grade, a pseudojoke circulated around the playground and stayed for what felt to us like an eternity—weeks, maybe months. The story was inevitably told with minor variations in background information and character development, and the setting was always shifting slightly from the North Pole to the South Pole, but the essential situation tended to remain largely intact: a male polar bear and a female polar bear live happily together on an ice floe until one day it splits apart. As Mama Polar Bear floats east and Papa Polar Bear floats west, Mama Bear calls out (and here it was vitally important to pronounce the punch line with just the right mix of interrogatory confusion and exclamatory fatigue), *"Radio!?"*

Several of us would watch as one of us told the joke to an uninitiated classmate, and when the punch line was delivered, we'd all laugh maniacally. The joke, of course, was that there was no joke, and the point was to prove how compliant all us sixth-graders were. The listener always followed our lead and laughed and laughed. The instant he started to laugh, we'd fall completely silent and ask, "What's so funny?"

"Well, you know," he'd say, still holding his stomach.

"No," we'd say, "tell us."

"Well, you know, '*Radio!*'"

Unpersuaded, we'd press him further, and he'd retreat to the position that it just sounded funny: the two polar bears, the ice floe, "*Radio!?*"

"What's funny about it?" we'd ask again.

And then he'd have to acknowledge that he laughed only because we were laughing. "Wasn't it supposed to be funny?" he'd ask.

Sooner or later we'd laugh at him and explain the situation and call him that most terrible name: "conformist." What we ignored for the most part was the process by which we had recently been introduced to the situation ourselves, and speaking strictly of myself for a moment, how comparatively late in the game I was allowed to be enlightened, occupying as I did the singular position of indisputably least popular person in the indisputably most popular group.

Blood and Guts in High School

In high school I was athletic and thus, to a certain extent, popular. However, I worked unduly hard at sports, with very little *sprezzatura*, which made me extremely unpopular among the dozen or so really popular, athletic people. Why? Because I made popularity or grace look like something less than a pure gift. Only the dozen or so really popular, athletic people knew I was unpopular, so I could, for instance, be elected, if I remember correctly (I don't: I'm making this up), vice president of the junior class and yet be, in a sense, underappreciated. It was a frustrating place to reign, really, consigned to the highest ring of the *Ringstrasse*, unable to escape or improve. Every Halloween I cowered in my basement bedroom with the doors locked, lights out, shades down, and listened to the sound of lobbed eggs.

In the fall of 1973 I broke my leg, badly, playing football on the beach (so Kennedyesque!), and the first day I was home from the hospital I lay immobile in a body cast in the living room, an aluminum pin in my thigh. Two medics carrying a stretcher stormed the front door, looking for someone who had supposedly fallen on the front steps. Later that afternoon, a middle-aged man, slightly retarded, tried to deliver a pepperoni pizza. A dump truck started pouring a ton of gravel into our miniscule backyard. A cop came to investigate a purported robbery. Another ambulance. A florist. An undertaker from central casting. A paint salesman. My popular, athletic friends, who had gathered together to watch the proceedings with binoculars in one of their houses at the top of the hill, orchestrated this traffic all night and deep into the morning.

They meant it as a terrorizing, thoroughly evil prank, and my mother certainly saw it that way (I was the only Jew among my jock friends, who nicknamed me "Buddha Boy"), but I never took it as anything other than the most moving, collective confession of the pain that consists of the inability to identify with someone else's pain other than by intensifying it. Vehicles from most areas of the service sector were parked, at one point, virtually around the block.

Always

Life, as the well-worn joke has it, is like high school, but with more money. Proof:

Four locutions are exceedingly popular among a certain group of well-educated, highly self-conscious people. One involves the use of the word "about." Things are never said to be about something; they are always said to be not about something. People say, for instance, "This isn't about your parents." What it is about, on the other hand, is never said, without the risk of acute embarrassment. To say exactly what something is about suggests an inability to entertain contradiction.

Another phrase is "hilarious." Almost everything is said to be hilarious. Never anything even slightly funny. "Hilarious" is shorthand for "exquisitely painful" or "emblematically mordant." Sometimes something sad happens, someone pronounces the occurrence "hilarious" to someone unfamiliar with this other, more sophisticated meaning of "hilarious," and the person saying something is hilarious when it isn't is greeted with a quizzical expression or a sock in the mouth.

The third phrase, used when the speaker is ostensibly searching for the right word, is "I want to say . . ."; the substituted word never even remotely resembles the word the speaker is looking for, and the speaker is always someone who worships at the altar of the sound of his own voice.

The final term is even more popular than "about" or "hilarious" or "I want to say . . . ." Whenever any kind of calamity occurs—a water main breaks, an earthquake, a hurricane, a volcano, passengers spill out onto the tarmac after a plane crash—it's always, always said to be "like a movie."

Almost Famous

But never, in my hearing, "like a Bob Balaban movie." A less robust Craig Wasson; a much more neurotic John Savage; Charles Martin Smith without his likable sanity.[4] Wallace Shawn sans self-deprecation—Bob Balaban is a character actor who looks like a balding baby wearing a beard and glasses. He is never not the quintessential shlemiel: In *Midnight Cowboy*, his debut film, he suffers five indignities in five minutes—hires Joe Buck to be the recipient of his blow job in a movie theater in Times Square; coughs and spits out Joe Buck's cum into the bathroom sink; doesn't have the money to pay Joe Buck ("I was lying"); offers Joe Buck his school books as payment; and pleads, successfully, with Joe Buck not to take his watch ("My mother will die").

In *Report to the Commissioner*, Balaban plays Joey Egan, a legless man scooting around Times Square on a board with wheels. Dogs attack him; he barks back and bites people's legs. After another cop, weary of "Crazy Joey"'s antics, tosses Joey's board into a dumpster, Michael Moriarty, who plays undercover detective Bo Lockley, rescues Joey's board for him. Later, Balaban hitches a ride on the rear bumper of a cab, trying to help Moriarty track down an evil pimp named Stick, but for his efforts only lands headfirst in a pile of garbage. Moriarty winds up apprehending the pimp in Saks, though Moriarty—a deeply flawed hero—later kills himself. Balaban doesn't kill himself; it would seem redundant.

Nowhere-man as bureaucrat:

In *Absence of Malice* Balaban plays Elliott Rosen, the head of a Justice Department special task force investigating Mafia links to organized labor in Miami. Though in most other movies he has a beard, here he has only a trim moustache. He wears a pocket protector for his many pencils and pens; speaks rapidly in a defeated, self-canceling manner; and constantly winds and unwinds a rubber band. He tricks plucky Sally Field and attempts to arraign hunky Paul Newman, so he winds up being fired by folksy Wilford Brimley.

In *Prince of the City* Balaban plays a prissy, patrician, and condescending Justice Department official in Washington prosecuting corruption among mostly Italian cops in New York City. He checks people's names off a list, which means he views their lives as abstractions. Wearing a bowtie, he dresses, talks, and acts like he's living in the wrong century: specifically, the eighteenth. As in *Absence of Malice*, he represents—in contrast to Italians, who possess joie de vivre and know how to dress—the disembodied intellect: he doesn't get what's life's about; he isn't in touch with elemental forces.

In *For Love or Money*, Michael J. Fox is Doug Ireland, a concierge at a fancy New York hotel who must choose between Christian Hanover—his very wealthy backer for a renovation project involving the transformation of an abandoned castle on Roosevelt Island into a luxury hotel—and Andy Hart, Hanover's beautiful mistress, who is falling in love with Fox. Hanover bribes Ed Drinkwater (Balaban, of course, that water drinker, who doesn't get that life is a glass of champagne from which to drink lustily) to investigate Fox for tax evasion, in order for Hanover to manipulate him into signing away the rights to the property. Balaban says, "I got Leona; I'll get you." Balaban says, "Nice car for a bellhop."

Balaban says, "You're in deep shit, Mr. Ireland." In a movie about love being more important than money, Balaban is, first and last, money.

The yuppie-swine motif:

In *Alice*, a lamentation on materialism, he concludes his marriage proposal to Mia Farrow by noting, "I have a lot of money."

Girl Friends honors, as do so many films Balaban is in, ambivalence (here, two women's choices of artistic career vs. marriage), and Balaban embodies, as he does so often, the end of ambivalence, the pejorative of the extreme position. He doesn't know how to participate in the give-and-take of the dialectic because he's the Scarecrow: no heart. He enters the movie—a man named Martin—daintily carrying finger food and correcting his wife's narration of their honeymoon slide show: Agadir, not Rabat. "When we go to Italy," he giddily exclaims, "we're going to write down everyone's sizes!" Fastidious, workaholic, yet with a perpetually distracted air, he sniffs, sneezes, smokes European cigarettes, favors the word "exquisite." The last line of the movie is him calling out, concernedly but pitifully, the name of his wife, the woman who has made the wrong decision—given up her poetry for marriage and motherhood. The two women look at each other and laugh. Balaban is the embodiment of the idea of husband as an early grave.[5]

In *Amos & Andrew*, Andrew Sterling, a Pulitzer Prize–winning black intellectual, buys a summer house on Martha's Vineyard, but the night he moves in, his white neighbors, Phil and Judy Gillman, mistake him for a robber. When the police chief, who is running for reelection, realizes that he and his officers have been shooting at a celebrity, he arranges for Amos—a recently arrested white "career criminal"—to take Andrew hostage and whisk him out of town before the truth can emerge. Surrounded by opportunistic black protesters and racist white summer people, Amos and Andrew bond and grow: the black man teaches the bumbling white man a little self-respect, while the white man teaches the uptight black man how to be a little more down. The film is about breaking out of self-pitying definitions of oneself as a victim. Balaban, a "criminal psychologist and freelance hostage-crisis counselor" whose name is a joke from elementary school (R. A. Fink), is counter-example as always: a self-absorbed hostage negotiator who spends the entire movie on the phone, bewailing his own microscopic moments of childhood pain: "I remember my eleventh birthday. I had a party. My mom and dad hired a clown. It was a very, very funny clown and it juggled, did magic tricks. My friend Ruby peed on the floor—she was really embarrassed—but I had a good time. And then the next year my mom called his house to hire him for my twelfth birthday party and his wife answers the phone and she says, 'I'm sorry, he's not a clown anymore. He's at school, learning how to be a dental technician.' I don't think I'll ever forget that moment."

On *Seinfeld*, he plays the president of NBC, who becomes infatuated with Elaine to the point of incapacitation. Attempting to impress her (she's utterly indifferent to him), he joins Greenpeace, and on his first assignment at sea, suffers death by drowning.

In *Whose Life Is It Anyway?*, playing an incompetent attorney, he stutters—occasionally and unconvincingly.

Techno-geek:

Little Man Tate is about a boy genius trying to find a balance between Dede, his working class mother who wants to give him a "normal" childhood, and Dr. Grierson, his overzealous tutor escorting him to the thirteenth annual "Odyssey of the Mind," a "mental Olympics" for prodigies. Balaban is the math contest emcee at Odyssey of the Mind. His first line is: "Another round of questions." There is life-giving emotion, the film means to say, and death-dealing intellection; Balaban represents the *via negativa*, the coldest star in the cosmos.

In *Catch-22*, Balaban plays bombardier Orr, a "one-man disaster area" whom Yossarian refuses to fly with, despite Orr's vow that he'll take "good care" of him. Yossarian pretends to be crazy, but Orr seems truly to be crazy: he wildly overdoes the thumbs-up sign when taking off, and in a sexual frenzy over Major Major's mistress, bites his headset. He bails out over the Mediterranean and Adriatic, crash-lands, drifts for days, gets picked up at sea. It's "good practice." What, with that goofy smile, does he know that we don't? *Catch-22* is the exception proving the rule: it's the only film in which Balaban even remotely triumphs, but, revealingly, his triumph is offscreen. The primary significance of Yossarian's discovery that Orr has made it—he rowed to Sweden (his name turns out to have been a prophetic pun)—is that it inspires Yossarian to break the impasse: he sets out in his own tiny dinghy into the enormous sea. In a film constructed across the loop-the-loops of paradox, Balaban is as rigid as reinforced steel.

In *Altered States* William Hurt is Faust: Eddie Jessup, a genius psychophysiologist who immerses himself in an isolation tank and digests blood and sacred mushrooms in order to try to discover the origins of human life.[6] Balaban—Arthur Rosenberg—is Jessup's literal-minded research assistant, who, when he helps Hurt out of the tank at the end of an immersion and says to him, "I'd like to try that sometime," transparently would not like to try that sometime. At a party at Balaban's apartment, his harridan wife tells him to go answer the door, at which stands William Hurt—in a halo of backlighting, the better to be admired by Blair Brown. Balaban's only gear is pedantically busyness: analyzing data, synthesizing drugs, fiddling with his bag lunch, "fractionating rat brains." Humble technician to Hurt's mystic seeker, he asks where the research is headed and is uncomfortable with Jessup's hip adventurousness: "We're just bootlegging." Did Faust have an errand boy? I can't remember, but I think he must have.

In *2010*, as Dr. R. Chandra, designer of the Hal 9000 computer, Balaban says, "Whether we are based on carbon or silicon makes no fundamental difference. We should each be treated with appropriate respect." The audience wonders exactly to what degree Balaban shares essential molecular structure with earthlings. As always, he's the foolish intellectual—adenoidal, aphysical, distant, unconnected to ordinary human emotion. Attempting to persuade a NASA official to allow him to bring Dr. Chandra with him on the mission, Roy Scheider says, "He designed Hal. He can reactivate him."

NASA: I think he *is* Hal.
SCHEIDER: I know.
NASA: Yeah, but can you trust him?
SCHEIDER: No, but I have to.

Balaban is happy only when talking to Hal, proud of Hal's ability to process "information without distortion or concealment." When, preparing to meet his doom, Hal asks, "Will I dream?" and Balaban answers, "I don't know," Dr. Chandra is crying.

In *Close Encounters of the Third Kind*, Balaban is "Interpreter Laughlin," a cartographer, or, as he explains to the audience, "a mapmaker." He's not a professional interpreter, but his French is good enough to explain things to Truffaut. Balaban is pure rational intelligence. "I don't believe it," he says at one point, over and over and over. "Why is it here?" When the UFO communicates, everybody is gaga, except Balaban, who points out that the UFO is conveying its latitude and longitude. When the UFO arrives, everybody takes an involuntary step forward—to enter the mystery—except Balaban, who stands still as a slide rule.

In Balaban's book, *Close Encounters of the Third Kind Diary*, one entry reads: "At the pool today Truffaut asks me if I wouldn't mind reading a script for him. He reads English very well, but someone has sent him a SciFi script, and he is having trouble understanding some of the technical terms. I am tremendously flattered and run up to my room to read it immediately. It's not a very good script, but I read it thoroughly and take copious notes; I want to give Truffaut an accurate report. Later he asks me what I thought. I fill him in on the story. I launch into an incredibly boring scene-by-scene synopsis. Truffaut listens very politely as I ramble on for fifteen minutes, retelling every trivial incident in the complicated script. I give possible meanings and interpretations for every twist and turn of its convoluted plot. . . . Finally he stops me. He smiles: 'Could you please just tell me if you think it's good or bad?'"[7]

In Our Hands, a documentary about the antinuke march in Central Park in 1982, includes short interviews with dozens of singers and actors. This is so perfect that it sounds like I'm making it up, but I'm not: Balaban, alone among his colleagues, goes unidentified.

What is Bob Balaban, anyway, a professional punching bag? What indignity will the movies not subject him to? What indignity will he not accept? What depth of self-loathing allows him to be used this way? What does it mean to have a face that the camera reviles? Couldn't his life count, too, along with the beautifully real—romantic, operatic, tragic—lives whirling around him? Could he ever see himself in romantic, operatic, tragic terms? What have these roles done to him?

Like someone dead or very famous, Balaban is trapped in an absolutely unchangeable identity.[8] In almost all of these movies he's extremely dislikable, and in almost all of the movies he's extremely dislikable in precisely the same way: humorlessly overconcerned with procedure, passive-aggressive to the point of self-parody, dogged, eunuchized, bloodless. Balaban frequently gives his character a peculiar habit: sneezing, stuttering, playing with his food, winding and unwinding a rubber band. It's difficult to believe that this is only a coincidence, that various directors just happened to give him a trick for us to remember him by. On the other hand, I find it even harder to think of Bob Balaban as Chekhov, knowing his character so well that he knows everything about him: how he eats, how he talks, what he does with his hands—as if these things somehow either excused us for despising him or explained something or other, as if the thing we hated about him weren't him, as if it were only this one particular flaw we couldn't abide. The technique distances Balaban from his character, his character from us: he doesn't want to be associated with his onscreen persona any more than we do. Balaban is there to appreciate the hero for us: through him we gravitate toward the mysteries, but only by first sloughing him off as our abject substitute, the viewer's least self, with his—with our—ordinary self-interest, self-doubt, wariness, weakness, cowardice, incompetence, homeliness. Balaban almost always plays Jews (all those Elliotts); he's a scapegoat Christ suffering for our one irredeemable sin: we are not movie stars, either.

The Nimbus of His Fame
Makes a Nullity of Us All

On a visit to Los Angeles, I'm sampling two new flavors at the Brentwood Häagen-Dazs when in walks O.J. Simpson with two very young guys in excellent shape. Seniors, say, on the USC football team—I don't know. O.J.'s not in excellent shape, not even in good shape, not even close. He's no longer a senior on the USC football team. The air conditioning is on.

I've liked O.J. since I was a kid, because my cousin, a UCLA grad, has always rooted, in a gloating, ungracious manner, against USC. None of us say anything now to O.J. There is shyness to our behavior, but there is also a smidgen of self-respect. There are maybe six or eight people in the store other than me and O.J. and his friends. Part of the tension is the sheer surprise of seeing O.J. ordering ice cream; I've never thought of him doing something so mundane and unhealthy. In a curious way, he's unwelcome or at the very least not wholly embraced; he's intruding a little, maybe, by participating in our slovenliness.

Gallantly (so I first think), O.J. seeks to purchase a woman's ice cream for her. She suddenly looks much prettier to me than she had before. O.J. winks at the two seniors on the USC football team, applies pressure to the crook of the woman's arm, recommends rum raisin. I remember thinking, very specifically, *O.J's kinda tarnishing his reputation here*; this was years before he took the Bronco out for a spin on I-5.

The woman smiles a smile that goes exactly so far and no farther, and says, "Thank you but no," looking at me, trying to get me in on this. But I can't. I don't. Suddenly I'm just standing there.

O.J. persists, reiterating his desire to buy an ice cream cone for her. It's like watching a famous suicidal accordion fold in on itself:

O.J. keeps nudging the woman up to the counter while she, impressively, impassively, keeps saying, over and over, "No thanks, O.J. That won't be necessary. I haven't quite decided yet."

Finally, when O.J. refuses to relent, she points at me and says, "My boyfriend's treating."

"Your boyfriend?" one of O.J.'s minions mutters, in O.J.'s defense. "*That man's* your boyfriend?"

The Cultural Contradictions of Late Capitalism

"I've never seen kids with so many pimples so young. You both eat too much chocolate—candy, cookies, ice cream. *Ach.* You're going to have a lot of trouble later on."

I have a very vivid memory of my father saying this to me and my sister, and although there was a definite element of truth in what he said—in fifth grade I already had to avoid red shirts because they had the effect of extending the field of my inflammation—I've often wondered what could possibly have mandated him to predict such a dismal future for his children. I mean, really: what would have been his motivation? Self-laceration taking the ritual form of infanticide? (He himself, of course, had had very bad acne as a teenager.) A father's laudable anger at his children's early expulsion from paradise? A discomfiting plea aimed at getting us to step up our remedial techniques? Who knows?

My sophomore year of high school my zit problem reached such catastrophic proportions that once a month I drove an hour each way to receive liquid nitrogen treatments from a superserious dermatologist in South San Francisco. His office was catty-corner to a shopping center that housed a Longs drugstore, where I would always first give my prescription for that month's miracle drug to the pharmacist. Then, while I was waiting for the prescription to be filled, I'd go buy a giant bag of Switzer's red licorice. Not the cheap cherry version so much in favor now, though. The darker stuff: claret-colored. I'd tear open the bag, and even if—especially if—my face was still bleeding slightly from all the violence that had just been done to it, I'd start gobbling the licorice while standing in line for the cashier. This may sound a little gooey, but, looking back, I'm hard-pressed now to see the licorice as anything other than some sort of Communion wafer—as if by swallowing the licorice, my juicy red pimples might become sweet and tasty. I'd absorb them; I'd be absolved. The purity of the contradiction I remember as a kind of ecstasy.

My senior yearbook photo was so airbrushed that people asked me, literally, who it was.

Well, time heals all wounds; so they say. This isn't even remotely true. Time passes, they say. This is true. Ten, twelve, fifteen years passed:

I crave a bag of claret-colored licorice and can't find one any-where, so I write to Switzer's, in St. Louis: whither the good licorice of yesteryear? "Per your inquiry," Bart Kercher, Quality Control Manager, writes back, "our St. Louis facility produces Switzer's licorice candy, Switzer's red candy, Good & Plenty candy, and Good 'n Fruity candy. The 'claret-colored' Switzer's candy which you speak of was produced by a 'batch' cooking operation. Our plant has been modernized and we currently have a continuous cooking system for greater candy uniformity."[9]

A couple of weeks later, a large envelope arrives, bearing Switzer's largesse—licorice whips, strips, bits, Good & Plenty. I rip open the bags and boxes and chew and chew.

Robert Capa, Misunderstood

If your picture wasn't any good, you're not standing close enough.

—ROBERT CAPA

Zits: a boundless topic. In 1975, when I was a sophomore in college, my aunt was friends with and—from the way he once pushed upon me some sort of reference book he compiled—must also have been dating a man who for years had been an editor of the *New York Times Magazine*. So I knew a bit before everyone else at school that the *Times Magazine* was planning a long piece about Brown's New Curriculum, which by then was quite old. Brown is a small campus and insular in the extreme. When a reporter and photographer showed up one week in the fall of 1975, their presence was immediately known and remarked upon. On the one hand, they were treated with almost a parody of blasé disinterest, whose purpose was to demonstrate how far we'd progressed beyond such mundane considerations as school spirit and self-promotion. On the other hand, from freshman orientation (which consisted primarily of people comparing Yale wait list stories) through senior commencement ceremonies (which, according to those who knew, lacked the rowdy irreverence of Wesleyan's), never, ever in my life have I encountered a more self-conscious and insecure group of individuals than the Brown class of '78. Then, again, maybe it was just me, insanely alert to rumors of my own inadequacy. There was, in any case, ambivalence toward the *Times* coverage—a certain feigned but felt indifference mixed with a childish hope that our parents back in the suburbs would read about the alarmingly bright Brown student body.

By the time the article came out, we'd forgotten all about it, and like any newspaper story whose subject you know well, it got things wrong and it was unbelievably boring. (My mother was a lifelong journalist and fan of Israel Shenker and S. J. Perelman;

still, when she read Shenker's portrait of Perelman in the *Times*,[10] she said, "Like every news story I've ever known anything about personally, it was a bummer: inept, too cute, biased, incomplete. It made me wonder about all those stories I've admired.") I don't remember much else about the article except that it appeared to have been written, in general, by the Brown admissions office, dwelling as it did upon the precipitous rise in the number of applications.

I do remember, however, the photographer taking picture after picture of me and my Classics classmate, Theodore "Tad" Kinney III, as we talked about who knows what outside Wayland Arch— probably how much better Tad Kinney was at Petronius than I was. I remember opening up the magazine and seeing the picture of Tad talking to . . . no one. As a sophomore in college I still had such acute acne that every night I had to mix and then wear a complex formula my dermatologist back in the Bay Area had prescribed for me; I didn't embody Brown's "new popularity" in the way that Theodore "Tad" Kinney III, with his tortoiseshell glasses and Exeter jaw, did. The point isn't that the Elephant Man always has some slight slight to complain about; the photo editor probably did me a favor by cropping me out of the picture. The point is that for the purposes of the accompanying photograph, I couldn't exist.[11]

Ted Polumbaum (The New York Times)

Love Is Not a Consolation

Fifteen years later: We so hope to experience, through our boys banging shoulder pads, an image of our own excellence. We want to win so badly. Our whole sense of civic pride and anguished consolation depends upon it. Living, as we do, in the remote Northwest, we need to know we are more successful—or, if not more successful, at least stronger—than the pussies in California. We are, in point of fact, bigger and stronger than they are, but they're faster than we are. On a fall afternoon, we lose the big game.

To me, it's all oddly reminiscent of the Brown-Harvard game for the 1974 Ivy League championship. I was at Brown; my friend Alan, who was at Harvard, said, years later (when he was my friend), referring to the game, "It really did seem as if the Harvard players were simply smarter, don't you think?" He said this without hauteur or, on the other hand, irony or embarrassment.

In the remote Northwest, we paint our faces purple and gold, we stand shirtless atop cars in the chilly rain, we overturn garbage barrels and light them, we hoot. And yet, lopsidedly, we lose the big game. They move the ball better than we do; they have a superior kicking game; they deserve to win. Alternatively, they get all the breaks. We're too tight. We want it too badly. Our identity depends too transparently upon our performance.

For reasons I still can't quite discern, students here don't hold hands, but the next day is warm for mid-December in the remote Northwest, and three-quarters of the student body suddenly appear to pair off, buying groceries together, going to Sunday matinees, clinging to each other desperately, looking far more attractive together than they have ever looked apart, as if to announce *Love is not a consolation. Love is a light.*

Desire

Is desire, then, a sort of shadow around everything? Whatever my sister had—in this case, the hit record *Trip to the Farm*—I, by definition, wanted, because it had attained this one quality: it was outside my consciousness. The moment I held it, my mind experienced it, so I no longer wanted it.

All week long my sister and I would think and talk about *Batman* or *Get Smart* or *The Addams Family*—whatever the show was that year—and on the night of the show we'd make sugar cookies and root beer floats, then set up TV trays; immediately after the show, we'd talk about how much we hated that it was over and what agony it was going to be to wait an entire week for it to be on again, whereas the show itself was usually only so-so, hard to remember, over before you knew it.

Senior year of high school my best friend and I, who were both virgins, had to spend at least one night a week hanging around the San Francisco Airport. Why? The dirty magazines they let us flip through at the newsstand and the sexy stewardesses tugging their luggage like pets, but more than that it was everybody marching with such military urgency to their destinations, as if everywhere—

everywhere in the world: Winnipeg, Tokyo, Milwaukee—were to be desired.

I admire the Boy Scout belt a friend of mine is wearing—I like the way it's a joke about uniformity at the same time it simply looks good—and when I ask where he got it, he says, to my astonishment, that it's his original Boy Scout belt: he still has it; he can still wear it; he's very skinny, stylish, good-looking. I never made it past the Cub Scouts and even there failed to distinguish myself; slipknots and shiny shoes have never been very high priorities for me. But now I want a Boy Scout belt and think it will be easy. I stop in at a Boy Scout office, where I'm told that BSA clothing and accessories can be purchased only by Scouts or troop leaders. I go so far as to schedule an interview for a troop leader position until, fearing accusations of pedophilia, I end the charade. Visits to several stores lead me to the boys' department of J. C. Penney, which carries Boy Scout uniforms in their catalogue and tells me I can order a belt. They call me when it comes in. I wear it once, maybe twice, with jeans, then toss it into the back of the closet.

The Nimbus of Their Fame
Makes a Nullity of Us All

There is, for most people, including myself, a mysterious appeal about men in uniform. A baseball card trade show is being held at the Scottish Rite Temple. Jose Canseco and Ken Griffey Jr. sign autographs (for fourteen and seven dollars, respectively) from eleven A.M. until one P.M. on a Saturday, and when I show up at around twelve-thirty, the first five words I hear come from people standing at the end of a line: "No more Griffeys—sold out." Griffey stands behind a table, signing autographs with a cast on his right arm, in visible discomfort and in complete silence. At the next table over, Canseco wears white shoes, a pink shirt, a huge gold cross, a dark bruise on his right hand, a pinkie ring, and a gold watch. All in all he looks to me like someone doing a decent impression of Elvis at midcareer. He doesn't talk to anyone, either.

"Please have your items out, ready to be signed, please," a trade show coordinator says every few minutes.

"Did he talk at all?" a father asks his son after his moment with Canseco. "Did he say anything?"

"What they better beware of is people so pissed off they don't bother to come back," one collector tells another. "I mean, we waited four hours for a Sandy Koufax down in Anaheim last month."

As Griffey's deadline nears, one boy cuts in line of another kid. Their fathers start trading elbows. "Don't tell me to calm down," one of the men keeps saying.

"Christ, we came all the way from Yakima," two boys' grandmother complains to the organizers. "Do we get a refund if we don't get Canseco's signature?"

She's assured that she will, and later when I talk to her and her grandsons, the older boy says that even though Griffey's autograph cost seven dollars, he told his friends it would cost nine. "I sorta rip them off," he explains.

"The younger boy doesn't do business with the cards yet," the grandmother says. "He's only seven."

"What are you looking at?" a dealer asks me. "You looking at the Strawberry, huh?"—a 1983 Darryl Strawberry rookie card. "That's a tough card, man. That's a tough card. That's mint. The guy next door's selling it for forty-five dollars. His card you can burn."

There are posters everywhere: Griffey ("The Kid"), Will Clark ("Will Power"), Andre Dawson ("The Hawk"), Mike Greenwell ("Gator Country"). The only picture of a woman anywhere is a poster of Miss Miami looking up admiringly at Canseco. Another kid is disappointed that Canseco didn't talk to him, and his mother responds, "Ooh, Canseco—that dark hair; did you see his eyes?"

A father tells me his son had "twenty-three Kevin Mitchell rookie cards and lost the binder at the airport." He then stage-whispers: "Probably stolen. It was in San Francisco."

Later on, a boy with an Astros cap shrieks, "Ken Griffey!" A crowd gathers, as everyone hopes maybe Griffey has returned to grace us with his broken-armed signature for a few more minutes. "I got it," Astros says, showing us the card. "I got it. That's ten bucks."

I ask a patrician-looking man whether he's associated with Thyberg Sports, which is sponsoring the show, and he says no, he's a real estate agent just here with his grandson. I try to get him to evoke that time when he was at play in the fields of his youth and Mel Ott would hit home runs for sick children and sign autographs on napkins at the neighborhood tavern. Granddad will have none of such romance. "Baseball cards have stepped up in class," he says. "Topps is listed on the Big Board now."

When I was a kid, growing up in the sixties, Topps was the only baseball card manufacturer. Now there are Fleer, Donruss, Score, and Upper Deck, which is the hottest card because it has the "best borders"—uneven brown and green stripes down the right side.

"The borders *are* kind of nice," I say, studying a card.

"Like a highway," one kid says.

"A highway? No, it's like the brown is the infield and the green is the outfield, don't you think?"

"I never thought of it like that," the kid says.

Someone tries to sell Ricky Kwan, the twelve-year-old proprietor of Ricky's Batting Circle, an "error card," but Ricky doesn't bite. "I'm not that into error cards," he says. "They don't sell unless they're a Juan Gonzalez or somebody."

Error cards tend to be either reverse prints of someone fielding the wrong way or "short prints" of someone who retired soon after the card was issued. A rumor persists that Upper Deck issues reverse negatives on purpose, since the Upper Deck partners are traders themselves and they hold onto error cards for their own collections.

"Sort of like insider trading," I say.

"Exactly," says Ricky Kwan.

The Tradition Is Here,
the Memories Are Waiting
Several More Sporting Events
in Search of a Sponsor

"Hi, I'm Eddie Payton. My brother, Walter, holds the all-time rushing record in the NFL. So lots of investment firms would love to tackle the job of managing his money. But one firm works just as hard for people like you and me: Dean Witter. They're helping me save on taxes and plan for the future. You see, with Dean Witter, you don't have to be a Super Bowl champion to be treated like one. You're somebody, at Dean Witter."

"[Eric] Gregg, as he details in his autobiography, appropriately titled *Working the Plate* (Morrow), written with Marty Appel, grew up in the Bottom, a bleak ghetto in Philadelphia, and strove to become only the third black umpire in major league history.

"'I always wanted to be somebody,' Gregg said at the restaurant table, 'and very few people in my neighborhood even dreamed of getting out. When I was thirteen, I told my family, "One day I'm going to be on television." My mother said, "The only way that'll happen is if you sit on it." I walked out of the room.'"[12]

One night, as I walk around Seattle-Tacoma Airport, I listen to a black porter say, as he helps an old white lady into a wheelchair, "Don't worry, you're in good hands with Northwest." It's impossible to hear him say this without hearing the echo and conflation of at least three different commercial entities: Allstate's famously inaccurate slogan; *Driving Miss Daisy*; and the long-running spot of Sam Singletary, a Delta ticket agent, performing Herculean feats in order to return a lost briefcase to a passenger just in time for his flight. "Sam Singletary is a Delta ticket agent in Atlanta," explains Judy Jordan, Assistant Vice President, Advertising and Sales

Promotion. "Even though he has the same last name, to our knowledge, he is not related to Mike Singletary of the Chicago Bears."[13]

On the way to Portland for game three of the 1990 NBA finals, the Detroit Pistons' private plane, *Round Ball One*, made an unscheduled stop in Billings, Montana, for fuel. Film footage showed a few Pistons—Mark Aguirre, Dennis Rodman, James Edwards—getting off the plane and walking across the tarmac toward a door to the small airport. At first, and for a surprisingly long while, there was no mad stampede through the door to pummel the Pistons. According to broadcaster Pat O'Brien, the Billingtonians were "waiting for Grandma and Grandpa, but they came to their senses and went out and got autographs." Forgetting about Grandma and Grandpa in order to pay homage to the Pistons constituted, in other words, evidence of a return to full consciousness. Pat O'Brien said, "The players said they really enjoyed meeting the people."

"I see it as the life of the athlete," the senior writer for the weekly sports magazine explained. "You have the rookie phenom. Then you have the athlete who isn't living up to expectations. That can be almost any time in the middle era there. Then you have the troubled athlete, through drugs or what have you. You have the reborn athlete, through the good woman, Jesus, physical fitness, surgery. And then you have the comeback story, which is probably our classic: where the guy's been out of it and he has the big comeback, and everybody loves that. And then you also just have the evil athlete, the one who is not what he is perceived to be, the good guy who's actually a bad guy. That takes a special kind of writer to be nasty like that. And then you have the hero as hero, like Joe Montana, where you just reiterate how great somebody is. You also have the nostalgia pieces and your flat-out news stuff and the opinion pieces where you get to say things at the back of the magazine or whatever, that can be however off-the-wall as you want them or as off-the-wall as they will let them be. Those are pretty much the formats; there really isn't anything else. And I know it's true, because you try to think of another way to write something and you can't."[14]

In 1975, Alan was a junior at Harvard, living in a co-op on Brattle Street somewhere. The other members of the co-op felt that, on the whole, Alan didn't express his real feelings often enough, and when he did express his real feelings often enough, he didn't cry often enough to accompany the real feelings he didn't express often enough. On the whole. Once, in graduate school, when we all had to say where we'd gone to college, Alan said, "Harvard. University. In Cambridge." Here he pointed, vaguely, in a northeasterly direction. "Massachusetts." Which only had the effect, of course, of underlining the fact that Alan had attended the one school in America that exists in everyone's imagination. The cofounder of the co-op was worried about Alan. One evening, she came into his room and hugged him quite hard when she saw that he had gotten so deeply in touch with his feelings that he was sitting alone virtually in the dark, crying. A little light came from the nineteen-inch black-and-white television set perched delicately atop Alan's dresser. Alan was crying because Carlton Fisk had just homered barely inside the left field foul pole to win the sixth game of the World Series. A lifelong Red Sox fan born and raised in Woodbridge, Connecticut, Alan was crying with joy and was released from his co-op contract over Christmas break.

My father was born and raised in Brooklyn; the only pure moral passion I've ever felt has been for the Los Angeles Dodgers, even though I grew up in the Bay Area: land of the Giants. My proudest possession as a child was a signed copy ("To Dave with best wishes—I hope your ambitions are reached") of Jackie Robinson's biography, which my father kept for me in a safe-deposit box. I never traded a baseball card of a Dodger, even if I had seven duplicates. Pictures of the Dodgers, obtained from Union 76 gas stations in Los Angeles, covered my bedroom walls, and I went to sleep by saying their names; my parents weren't allowed to stop anywhere else for gas when we visited L.A. I hated Vin Scully, the Dodger announcer, because, unlike every other team's announcer, he prided himself on appearing neutral. The Dodgers were the embodiment of good, and the Giants were the embodiment of evil, and this was manifest in a myriad of ways: the name of the Giants' manager, Alvin Dark; the typical Giant's more threatening mien (Cepeda, Marichal, Mays, McCovey, the Alous, et al.); their very name, "Giants," which evoked their monstrousness, in contrast to "Dodgers" (trolley dodgers), whose image of vulnerability I loved; the Giants' ghoulish black-and-orange uniforms compared to the Dodgers' seraphic blue-and-white; their windy "Park" compared to our warm, sunny "Ravine" (located on Elysian Park Avenue). The first thing I did every morning of baseball season was go read the box score, and if the Dodgers had lost, I'd wail and wail, whacking my Frosted Flakes all around the breakfast room with my spoon. One of the few times I've ever told my father "I love you" was after he stayed up late with me, on April 21, 1987, listening to Mike Marshall hit a three-run homer in the tenth inning to beat the Giants. Whenever I hear mention, in any context, of the years 1955, 1959, 1963, 1965, 1981, or 1988, I think one thing: victory.

The kicker made the field goal, and as the game went to commercial, the kick was shown again in slow motion. The camera was positioned in such a way that the ball kept spinning higher into the upper-right-hand corner of the screen. At the end of the replay the ball was out of view, and for a held moment the screen showed only black, on a Monday night, November 6, 1989, in San Francisco, shortly after the earthquake. Then graphics came up. For a second or two, though, there was just the night in all its elegiac beauty. The shot conveyed terror, but only for a moment. Then graphics came up.

Always

The teaser for the sports highlights always shows everything up to but not including the conclusion of the play. If a coach is described as "classy" or "a class act," it always means he's achieved an erasure of personality so extreme that he can scarcely be said to exist. Asked to reveal the game plan for tomorrow, the player always says, "We're just going to go out and have fun." At the beginning of the all-star game, the sportscaster always says that the players just want to have fun today; at halftime, or in the bottom of the fifth inning, the sportscaster always says that the players' competitive spirit has taken over and now they all really want to win. Informed that the player feels great, the sportscaster always asks the player how he feels. Athletes who before the biggest game of their life say that they're not nervous at all always perform miserably. Asked how it felt to hit the game-winning shot, the hero of the game always says, "Words can't begin to describe how I feel." (Similarly, people who are obliged to write a thank-you note but who are unaccustomed to or uninterested in thinking in language always say, "I can't begin to express how grateful I am.") Curiously, though, athletes homing in on an especially elusive personal or team accomplishment are always said to care suddenly and inordinately about something called "history." The sportscaster, especially if he had a mediocre athletic career, always employs, as his only mode of rhetoric, a sort of hyper-attack jargon difficult to differentiate from a permanent sneer. Presented with the mildest of coincidences, the sportscaster always insists upon seeing poetic justice or delicious irony. If the play-by-play man doesn't understand what the color man just said, the play-by-play man never asks the color man what in the hell he's talking about.

After a career-ending injury, the athlete always says that he had always seen sports as just a stepping-stone to spreading the word of God. The passage advertised on a placard at a sporting event is always either Romans 10:9 or John 3:16. Once, at an Angels-Mariners game I saw on TV, a John 3:16 guy sitting near home plate in perfect position for the centerfield camera watched himself on a portable television and made constant, minute adjustments in the placement of his sign until a foul pop nicked him on the wrist.

Television stations always silently ID themselves at the most triumphal moment of the broadcast. Local affiliates always promote their eleven o'clock news by talking over the music as credits roll for network dramas ending at 10:55, lending the network dramas the ersatz poignancy of a national collective dream giving way to regional reality. Criminals being taken into custody always shield their face from cameramen. The sound cut never lasts longer than six seconds.[15] Male anchors always accomplish the segue from weather to sports by making a sort of pun, at which female anchors always feign amusement.

A TV movie is always based upon a true story, always features actors and actresses who are more attractive than their real-life models, and is always less well-structured than the true story upon which it is based. The producers of sitcoms are always Jewish, the shows are always based on their own childhoods, and there is never anywhere in the show even a trace of their ethnicity except for an ancillary character who hates himself. Whenever a character on a sitcom develops even the mildest following, the story editors, attempting to capitalize on his newfound popularity, always overemphasize his one truly charming trait or mannerism to such a degree that his personality no longer makes even the slightest sense, and whatever real appeal he once possessed is completely obliterated. Thus, when actors who will never not be synonymous with a single (putatively comic) role on a particularly successful television program appear on talk shows, they always talk very seriously about how boxed in they feel by the one image people have of them. But whenever an actor gives a decent line reading, it is always said, by way of praise, that he "really became his character," e.g., while driving to the studio every morning, talked to himself in the ship captain's rich, deep brogue. On the other hand, actresses who are known exclusively for their good looks always find a vehicle in which their characters are placed in distress and made up to look not so great; the week of broadcast, they always appear on talk shows to discuss how they aren't really that beautiful in the first place, how grueling makeup was every morning during the shoot, and how proud they are of the film and, in particular, their own contribution to it.

In movies, people with thin faces are always good, and people with round faces and/or bald heads are always either pathetic, wrong, or comical, but people with extremely thin faces are always wicked. In movies, Jewish characters can be many things—wits, cowards, whiners, geniuses, villains, accountants—but they are never one thing: the embodiment of the life force, who is always an Italian. In movies, suburbanites and yuppies always drive Volvos and always wind up learning that life involves compromise, pain, and loss. In movies, in contests between thoughtful analysis and inchoate feeling, inchoate feeling always wins out, e.g., "I will always, always, always be in love with Anastasia."

Whenever a comedian directs his first movie, he always spends days, nights, and weekends in the editing room, his friends always explain to him that he must choose between wanting a life or wanting a career, and he always—lugubriously, like Chaplin in Limelight—chooses a career.[16] When people meet a movie star, they are inevitably disappointed because she is always either a) indistinguishable from how she appears on screen, in which case the rationale for her enormous salary is difficult to discern; or b) completely different from, i.e., not as rambunctious as, her public persona, in which case she's thought to be a bit of a bore and a hypocrite. The second female lead in Woody Allen's annual movie has always just been very interesting in someone else's movie, is considerably less interesting in his movie, and is unlikely to do anything interesting ever again. The prerelease publicity for a major Hollywood movie always seeks to draw and sustain a parallel between the (sororal, fraternal, sexual, maternal, or paternal) psychodynamic on the set and the (sororal, fraternal, sexual, maternal, or paternal) psychodynamic of the plot. When people swoon over a movie and don't know what else to say about it, they always praise its production values.

"Media" is always singular. The West is always, from an eastern perspective, "out west." The East is always, from a western perspective, "back east." The Northwest is always either "the great Northwest" or "the remote Northwest," but never "the great and remote Northwest." The new trend in apparel—flannel shirts, torn jeans, overalls, glasses, hightops, unlaced laces—is always based upon clothes worn by unpopular people in previous decades. The "sixties" are always a monolith, from which the same banners always fly. The cover of every "women's magazine" that refers the reader inside to an article about a celebrity miracle diet will also always refer the reader inside to a recipe for chocolate cheesecake. Titles of articles in magazines always allude to titles of current movies, shows, songs, and, occasionally, books.

The creative process is always depicted as an unfathomably mysterious, unbearably grueling endeavor, and writers are always depicted (always depict themselves) as beautiful losers stumbling around in the metaphysical night, for which the ur-text is: "We work in the dark—we do what we can—we give what we have. Our doubt is our passion and our passion is our task. The rest is the madness of art."[17] System-destroying visionary geniuses always have the highest number of acolytes whose entire identity derives from the fact that they are followers of the visionary genius's system.[18] The penultimate praise for a novelist is that he shows "compassion" for his characters. The only higher praise is that she "loves" her characters. Writers are always said to be guided by these characters, and this always takes the following form: "I didn't know 'Mr. Blonde' had that knife in his boot until he pulled it out."[19]

Male book critics in major metropolitan areas are always rabid baseball fans. If a growing-up novel is told in the first-person, it is always—with or without any cause for comparison—compared to *The Catcher in the Rye*. When critics have absolutely nothing to say about Writer X's sixth novel, they always say that it "burnishes" Writer X's reputation. Political ideologues on both the right and left always reserve their deepest passion for detective novels.

American writers residing in and writing about the tristate area are always understood to be adumbrating a universal spiritual condition, whereas writers residing in and writing about the other forty-seven states are always congratulated for being gifted regionalists. Writers always say, "Show, don't tell." Writers always say they don't read their own reviews. Forced by social circumstance to praise novels they haven't read, writers always say they are "wonderfully evocative." Writers who write in a nondescript style about doleful individuals always cite, as an enormous influence upon their work, the short stories of Anton Chekhov. Writers who complain most vociferously about the way their work has been pigeonholed because of a particular personal attribute—their race, say, or sexual orientation, or even their physical beauty—are always the writers whose work (the reception to whose work) has most directly benefited from this attribute. Whenever every other avenue for publicity for a best-selling author's new book has been exhausted, the publicity then focuses on the demands and rigors of the publicity tour itself. Writers who are most eloquent on the subject of the death of the novel are always writers who were once mildly popular and now are no longer read.

The Confessions

In the *Confessions*, Rousseau writes: "The mere idea of all the usages of society—which it is so necessary to observe, and of which I am certain to forget one or other—is enough to frighten me." Rousseau forgets what he wants to forget. He'd like to forget the civilizing purpose to which language is subjected by society, but he thoroughly comprehends the relation between small talk and social compromise. Language is the last thing that he has and the one thing that is all his, but, of course, it's not his at all.

"In conversation, in order to speak to the purpose," Rousseau says, "it is necessary to think of a thousand things at the same time and at once." Rousseau doesn't want to speak to the purpose; he wants to write until he discovers a purpose. He doesn't want to be thinking of a thousand things at the same time while he's speaking; he wants to be thinking of nothing at all so that he can begin to write. For Rousseau, conversation is antithetical to writing. He says that "those who live in the world" must "make sure of saying nothing which can give offense." And yet one of the essential if undeclared purposes of the *Confessions* is to offend those who live in the world, to disaffect readers in order to win more profound sympathy from them later on.[20]

The Cultural Contradictions
of Late Capitalism

People who pay thirty-five dollars for vanity plates are, undoubt-edly, on the whole, less concerned with the fate of the earth than those who don't buy vanity plates, and yet the thirty-five-dollar fee is earmarked for the Environmental Protection Agency. If the lyrics are sad, the music is invariably upbeat; if, somehow, both the lyrics and music are sad, the video is upbeat. Sentimentality always covers hostility; morality always screens voyeurism, e.g., "Tonight's topic: rescuing transsexual teenage prostitutes"; the camera is always doing first to the damsel-in-distress's ass what the bad-guys-in-the-plot are judged in the harshest possible terms for trying to do. Plas-tic garbage bags are sold on the basis of their utility for people who want to walk around hilltops picking up soda bottles. Dry / Beer. Siskel / Ebert. I tend to like it when commercially successful people such as Frank Deford or Burt Reynolds pine, completely disingenu-ously, for the execution in their lifetime of one monumental work— a novel or movie "that lasts"—while I tend to hate it when James L. Brooks or Williams graduates starring in soap operas or JoBeth Williams go on and on about the Sturm und Drang of the creative process.

Such binary oppositions are stupid and old-fashioned; I know that. Jean-Jacques Rousseau knew that. Still, everything I hear, everything I see, seems to feature exactly the same collision: Gap ads featuring semicelebrities you feel guilty for either recognizing or not recognizing, fish-out-of-water-movies, buddy movies, Jekyll-and-Hyde movies, stage names combining the exotic and familiar. The first question I always ask whenever I play Twenty Questions is, "Famous or not famous?" and people always give me this pained look, like, Why even ask?

Almost Famous

My father's birth certificate reads "Milton Shildcrout." His military record says "Milton P. Schildcrout." When he changed his name in 1946 to Shields, the petition listed both "Shildkrout" and "Shildkraut." His brother Abe used "Shildkrout"; his sister Fay's maiden name was "Schildkraut." Who cares? I do. I want to know whether I'm related to Joseph Schildkraut, who played Otto Frank in *The Diary of Anne Frank* and won an Academy Award in 1938 for his portrayal of Alfred Dreyfus in *The Life of Emile Zola*.

I grew up under the distinct impression that it was simply true—the actor was my father's cousin—but now my father is considerably more equivocal: "There is the possibility that we're related," he'll say, "but I wouldn't know how to establish it." Or: "Do I have definite proof that he was a cousin of ours? No." Or: "My brother Jack bore a strong resemblance to him; he really did." From a letter: "Are we really related, the two families? Can't say for certain. What's the mythology I've fashioned over the years and what's solid, indisputable fact? I don't know." "We could be related to the Rudolph/Joseph Schildkraut family; I honestly believe that."

In 1923, when my father was thirteen, his father, Samuel, took him to a Yiddish theater on the Lower East Side to see Rudolph Schildkraut substitute for the legendary Jacob Adler in the lead role of a play called *Der Vilder Mensch* (*The Wild Man*). Rudolph was such a wild man: throughout the play, he hurtled himself, gripping a rope, from one side of the theater to the other. After the play, which was a benefit performance for my grandfather's union—the International Ladies Garment Workers—my grandfather convinced the guard that he was related to Rudolph Schildkraut, and he and my father went backstage.

In a tiny dressing room, Rudolph removed his makeup and stage costume, and he and Samuel talked. According to my father, Rudolph said he was born in Romania, and that later in his acting career he went to Vienna and Berlin. He and his wife and son, Joseph, came to New York around 1910, went back to Berlin a few years later, and then returned to the United States permanently in 1920. (Joseph Schildkraut's 1959 memoir, *My Father and I,* confirms that these dates are correct, which only proves that my father probably consulted the book before telling me the story.[21]) Samuel asked Rudolph whether he knew anything about his family's antecedents—how and when they came to Austria. Rudolph said he knew little or nothing. His life as an actor took him to many places, and his life and interest were the theater and its people. The two men spoke in Yiddish for about ten minutes; my father and grandfather left. What little my father couldn't understand, my grandfather explained to him later.

"For weeks," my father told me, "I regaled my friends and anybody who would listen that my father and I had visited the great star of the Austrian, German, and Yiddish theater in America— Rudolph Schildkraut. What's more, I said, he was probably our cousin. Nothing in the conversation between my father and Rudolph Schildkraut would lead me or anybody else to come to that conclusion for a certainty, but I wanted to impress friends and neighbors and quickly added Rudolph and Joseph Schildkraut to our family. I said, 'They're probably second cousins.' Some days I made them 'first cousins.' Rudolph Schildkraut, as you know, went on to Hollywood and had a brief but successful motion picture career. I told everybody he was a much better actor than his countryman Emil Jennings."

In 1955, my parents were living in Los Angeles, my mother was working for the ACLU, and my mother asked my father to ask Joseph Schildkraut to participate in an ACLU-sponsored memorial to Albert Einstein, who had died in April. "After all," my father wrote in reply to one of my innumerable requests for more information, "Einstein was a German Jew and Pepi [Schildkraut's nickname] had spent so much of his professional life in Berlin and was a member of a group of prominent people who had fled Germany in the years before Hitler and lived in the Pacific Palisades–Santa Monica area."

My father got Schildkraut's phone number and called him, telling him he was a Schildkraut, too, and inviting him to speak at the memorial tribute. "After much backing-and-filling and long, pregnant pauses (his, not mine) on the phone," my father said, Schildkraut told my father to bring him the script. A few days later my father went to Schildkraut's house in Beverly Hills to show him the script he would read at the memorial if he decided to appear on the program. Schildkraut came to the door, greeting Shields (né Schildkraut) stiffly. "He was very businesslike—cold, distant, is more like it." For a moment or two they talked about their families. My father told him about the backstage visit in 1923. Joseph knew absolutely nothing of the Schildkraut family's ancestry. "Joseph Schildkraut, I would say," my father said, "and I think it's a fair statement, was somebody who didn't think about his Jewish background."

Schildkraut talked to my father for about thirty minutes in the foyer of the big, rambling house. "Later, in telling the story, I often exaggerated—said he clicked his heels, Prussian-like. He really didn't." Schildkraut said that he had to show the script to Dore Schary for approval. (Schary was a writer who had become the head of production at RKO and then MGM. Anti-Communist fears lingered; the blacklist was still in effect.) Schildkraut told Shields to come back in a week.

When my father returned, Schildkraut again talked with him rapidly in the foyer of the house—"On neither visit did he have me come into the living room, nor did he introduce me to his wife, who was moving about in the next room"—and wound up saying that Schary had read the script and said it was all right. The script was taken almost entirely from Einstein's writings on civil liberties, academic freedom, and freedom of speech. The memorial was held at what was then the Hollywood Athletic Club and later became the University of Judaism. Also on the platform were Linus Pauling; A. L. Wirin, the chief counsel to the ACLU; John Howard Lawson, a screenwriter and the unofficial spokesman for the "Hollywood Ten"; Anne Revere, who before being blacklisted won an Academy

Award as best supporting actress for her performance as Elizabeth Taylor's mother in *National Velvet*, and a novelist who my father insists was once famous and who in any case has a name worthy of the Marx Brothers—Lion Feuchtwanger.

The event was free. Every seat in the immense auditorium was filled. Hundreds of people sat in the aisles. Eason Monroe, the executive director of the ACLU and a man upon whom my mother had an immense, lifelong crush, asked the overflow audience to find seats or standing room in several small rooms upstairs. Monroe assured them that all the speakers would come upstairs to address them after speaking in the main auditorium. The program started a little late, about eight-thirty P.M., but Schildkraut still hadn't shown up. Monroe asked Shields, "Milt, where's your cousin? It's getting late." My father assured Monroe he'd be there. "He was too big a ham to stay away on such an occasion." His name had appeared prominently in the ads as one of the main speakers.

Finally, Schildkraut showed. Monroe greeted him and asked him if, as the others had consented to do, he would also speak to the groups upstairs. Schildkraut said that first he'd speak to the main auditorium audience; then he'd "see."

The other speakers—Pauling, Wirin, Lawson, Revere, and Feuchtwanger—spoke to the audience in the main auditorium, were "warmly received" (whatever that means), then went upstairs to speak once again to the overflow audience in a couple of ante-rooms. "The occasion lifted even the most uninspired speaker and material to emotional heights," according to my father. "But then came Pepi, the last speaker on the program. When he got to the podium, the audience was noisy and restless. After all, people were feeling the emotion of the memorial to this great man. Schildkraut took one look out there and employed the actor's stratagem: he whispered the first line or two, and a hush fell over the audience. Then, when he was sure he had their attention, he thundered the next lines. When he finished, he got a standing ovation. And this for a political naïf, or worse: a man who certainly didn't agree with everything he had just read, or anything else Einstein stood for. But he was the consummate actor and he read his lines—to perfection."

When Schildkraut finished, my father asked him about going upstairs. Schildkraut looked right through Shields and walked out the door. "Now he truly was like a Prussian soldier. That's the last time I saw him. In person, that is. Of course, I saw *The Diary of Anne Frank* on the screen half a dozen times. And if it's ever on television, I watch it again."

Fifteen or twenty years later my half-sister, Emily, was working as a maid at a motel in Oregon. "Don't know how it happened," my father explained, "but Pepi and his wife were guests at this posh place." Emily introduced herself, told him who she was, and Schildkraut gave her one of his "stylish Borsalino felt hats, which he wore in rakish over-one-eye European style—always the matinee idol—as a souvenir." She gave the hat to my father, who "had it in the closet for years, but it must have got thrown out when I moved after your mother's death."

I tell this story to Emily, who writes back: "Concerning the story about Joseph Schildkraut giving me a hat—that's a total mystery to me! I did work for a short time in a hotel in Cannon Beach, Oregon. I have no memory of this mysterious visitor—or even seeing him—except in the movie *The Diary of Anne Frank*. Either I was that spaced-out in those days and have blocked out this significant event, or once again our Pop has fabricated another yarn for you from his rich imagination. Sorry."

I relay what Emily has said back to my father, who wants to know: "Then where did the Borsalino hat come from? I distinctly remember Emily telling us that when she learned Joseph was a guest at the Oregon resort she was working at, she went over to him, told him her father's original name, they talked for a few minutes, and then Pepi gave her the hat. He wore hats like a Borsalino in his stage and screen roles back in the days when all male actors wore hats. And Borsalino, an expensive Italian-made hat, would be his style."

Then, shortly afterward, in a truly weird coincidence, an old friend of our family's calls my father and asks him to pick up two boxes of odds and ends that my father had left with them many years ago. "The lid flipped open on one of the boxes, and on top there was the hat Schildkraut gave to Emily at that Oregon coast resort back in the early seventies. Thought you'd be interested to learn about my (accidental) archaeological finding."

I am, I am, but the hat proves nothing. Only very recently I happened to discover that Schildkraut died in 1964, which means that Emily—sweetly seeking my father's appreciation—must have invented the entire story, my father invented the story, I've got the details wrong, or being in a family is indistinguishable from playing telephone. And yet the photograph in *My Father and I* of Schildkraut kissing Susan Strasberg on the forehead in *The Diary of Anne Frank* mimics exactly the overwrought staginess in two photographs of my father kissing Emily when she was very little. In so many photographs of "Pepi" or my father or me is this certain quality of mugging hungrily, of pretty-boyness (me till I was twelve, my father deep into middle age ["Your dad is a really distinguished looking man!"], Schildkraut until he was dead), of stilted posedness, of on-your-knees-before-the-camera obsequiousness, of needing to be liked by the lens, of peasant smilingness, of overreliance upon previous modes of appearing in pictures. . . .

Schildkraut also has what is to me a disturbing-because-familiar detachment toward his own feelings. "Maybe there was no such thing as love in real life," he writes. "These all-consuming agonies and ecstasies of love existed only on the stage."[22] I once wrote about stuttering that "it prevents you from ever entirely losing self-consciousness when expressing such traditional and truly important emotions as love, hate, joy, and deep pain. Always first aware not of the naked feeling itself but of the best way to phrase the feeling so as to avoid verbal repetition, you come to think of emotions as belonging to other people, being the world's happy property and not yours—not really yours except by way of disingenuous circumlocution."[23]

The tightest warp and woof I can weave comes from the sound of the syntax. Joseph says of Rudolph: "He was passionately in love with the sound of words. They intoxicated him." Joseph says of his mother: "She had an acute business sense, a talent for making every kreuzer count."[24] My father says: "You can bet all the borscht in Brownsville on that." My father writes: "It's been at least a year since that coffee-klatch-cum-current-events-discussion-group held its final meeting, but many people at Lakewood Village still talk about the explosive events of that fateful day." I write: "The tightest warp and woof I can weave comes from the sound of the syntax." Do you hear the keynote—the incessant buzz and hum of alliteration? I point out to my father what I see as the link between Schildkraut's alliteration-dependent writing style, my father's style, and my own (as well as my stutter), and he writes back: "About Joseph Schildkraut's style: I believe the book he wrote in collaboration [*My Father and I*, "as told to Leo Lania"] is the only thing he's ever written. Solo, or with somebody's help. Don't know how much his collaborator did and what Pepi contributed. My style? Strictly journalese. Marked—riddled?—by too much, far too much, alliteration. The O. Henry influence: as a young boy of seven or eight, I read his stories over and over. My brother Phil had won a complete set of O. Henry in a writing contest and there they were for me to devour—and (sadly) to incorporate, lock, stock, and barrel, into my own writing."

I tell my father that I hope to travel some day to Eastern Europe to trace the Schildkraut ancestry, and he responds: "That would be a dream trip—you and me investigating the Schildkraut strain in Austria, Germany, and the Ukraine. Whenever you're ready, I'll be ready. It would be a great adventure." I explain that what I'm most interested in is my need to get him to tell the stories over and over and over again and his ceaseless capacity to reinvent and extend the material. He replies (and this is what I've come to recognize as my father's signature and see projected forward in myself and backward in Schildkraut: an unshakable self-consciousness), "Writing about it, you'll probably use and exploit how I arrogated to myself the 'cousins, yeah, they're probably second cousins' relationship. And how I told and retold—dined out a lot on it, as the saying goes—the story of my one actual involvement, in person, with Pepi: the Einstein memorial night, etc."

Well, so, as my father likes to say, what? What is this correlation-seeking but a ghoulish attempt to backform a bloodline to star power? What proof is it, in any case, to find common traits in a putative relative's memoir? Is he or isn't he? Was he or wasn't he? I don't know, I can't know, and I'll never know; why, then, is it important for me to believe there's a link? Why do I care about being related to someone who—on the basis of my father's stories and *The Diary of Anne Frank*—appears to be a singularly unpleasant human being and painfully ham-fisted actor?[25] Because, as Sting says, "in America, everybody is in show business and nobody isn't an actor. Everyone is aware of the camera, whether it exists or not, and everybody aspires to be famous."[26] Star-fucker: name-dropper: strain-strainer. My father now informs me that he believes—although he can't be absolutely certain—that we're related to Robert Shields (né Schildkraut), of the former San Francisco mime duo Shields & Yarnell, and I can't help it: I think, well, then, maybe I'm also related to Brooke Shields; toward the end of *Endless Love*, when she's crying in that dark New York hotel room, trying to say goodbye to David, and her hair is braided and rolled up in a bun, she does, it seems to me, especially in the mouth and chin area, look at least a little the way I sometimes looked as a teenager. . . .

The Nimbus of His Fame
Makes a Nullity of Us All

My sister and I were just kids in 1965—ten and nine, respectively—when an article about our half-brother, Joseph, my father's son from his first marriage and named for Joseph Schildkraut, appeared on the front page of the Saturday *San Francisco Chronicle*. Joseph has always been the hippest person I've ever known. Walt Disney's death, he once informed me, was the greatest day in American cinema. His three favorite movies are *Terminator*, *Thief*, and *2001*: all attitude. He once did a U-turn in a kelly-green Triumph (with me in it) across an eight-lane highway. He's always seemed very male (as a child he went in for all the sheriff's costumes and Lone Ranger outfits that never had much appeal for me), endearingly vague, elegant, handsome, and cheerful, if a bit smug.

Now he edits teasers for *Jeopardy* and other shows, but in 1965 he was a senior at Berkeley, and according to the article on the front page of the *Chronicle*, "part of a vast and busy University of California drug peddling operation." The article was headlined "Big UC Campus Drug Case—Hunt for 'Mr. Big.'" Joseph wasn't Mr. Big—"allegedly a Berkeley campus source of large quantities of narcotics and so-called mind-expanding drugs such as LSD and DMT"—but it was clear he was on speaking terms with Mr. Big: "Officers went to Shields's apartment at 1709 Channing Way and found therein, they said, 720 ampules of DMT with an estimated market value of $1500." The usual retro pleasures are present when reading an old newspaper article:

> A meeting had been arranged for yesterday at which Detro and Jimenez were to buy $10,000 worth of LSD from Mr. Big. But Mr. Big failed to appear and had, in fact, vanished.
>
> Jimenez and Detro recalled that during one of their early meetings in the San Pablo Avenue bar, Mr. Big had demanded that they put up part of the money in advance. They refused.
>
> "Well, like, man, I don't know you guys," Mr. Big replied, "and you could be narcos (police). You know, the State got 50 new undercover men."
>
> Jimenez answered, "I never heard of a bust (arrest) at UC."[27]

At the time, though, Joseph had to reassure my father that he was completely innocent—he had no idea what his roommates were doing with all those glass ampules; he thought it was part of some lab experiment—and my sister and I had to worry all weekend about what taunts would greet us at school on Monday. (Summer school: what grinds we were.) The funny thing was that no one, not friends or fellow students or teachers or the principal, seemed to have seen the article, or if they did see it, they didn't connect it to us, or perhaps they simply had the grace not to wonder aloud (it's a common enough name, I suppose, and we've never looked that much alike, Joseph and I.) So what I did after several days of silence—and I've never known whether my sister did the same; we weren't prone to compare notes about this kind of an event—was to bring several copies of the article to school and wave them in people's faces and bemoan the family tragedy of it all and in that way glean at least a little glamour from the guilt by association.

Lynch/Frost Productions

Robert Capa, Misunderstood

In his diminutive, hawkish handsomeness, he looks a lot like Joseph looked in his twenties. His method of operation is virtually unvarying and, in its own way, brilliant. First, he asks you how many murders you've committed recently ("Just a rough estimate; I know it's hard to keep track"), how many adulterous affairs you are currently having ("You're married, aren't you?"), whether he hasn't seen your picture somewhere recently ("In the post office perhaps?"). Then he asks you how many bodies you've seen wash up on shore this week, how many of your friends are drug addicts, whether this isn't the mass-murder-and-adultery capital of the country. Finally, he asks whether you haven't been watching *Twin Peaks* ("Isn't everything you see on TV true?"), whether real life isn't in fact much more exciting and corrupting than television ("Is the American public being deceived?").

Mike Watkiss, a reporter for the television show *A Current Affair*, strolls around Snoqualmie with a cameraman, a sound man, and a production assistant, interrogating people. After hanging around with them for an hour or so, I reluctantly agree that it seems at least plausible that this is what they say it is: "just a light piece." My reluctance has to do with the fact that I have no idea how the footage will be edited, nor do the people being interviewed, and our uncertainty (*this guy's not serious, is he?*) is the very quality that gives the interviews their baffling imbalance. Still, as Watkiss says, he's been told to come up here and have a look around, but it's obvious "this town is, like someone in that *Star* article said, a lot more like Mayberry than Twin Peaks."²⁸ They're just having some fun with it.

Like most male movie stars (Al Pacino, Dustin Hoffman, Sylvester Stallone, Tom Cruise), Watkiss is quite short and, seemingly as a result, has extremely fine, extremely telegenic features: prominent cheekbones, dramatic eyes, a strong chin, an amazing amount of dark hair. He seems to be an emissary not so much from New York or L.A. as from television itself.

Watkiss's approach is mock melodramatic, pseudoconspiratorial: tabloid journalism taken to parody. "You'd have to be brain-dead to take this seriously," he explains. Cool presence, coruscating irony—at first, these seem to be the principal techniques by which Watkiss dominates his subjects. No one can even remotely resist his presence. A relaxed hipster on a bicycle says how much he wants to be interviewed, but when asked on camera how many adulterous affairs he's having, he suddenly tenses up and laboriously explains that he's single. His giddy friend, asked how many murders he's committed this week, becomes oddly solemn and starts talking about the Defense Department and being a survivalist. Two police officers find themselves denying, through pursed lips, that Snoqualmie is the mass-murder capital of the country. A bright, bespectacled young woman turns a little shrill and accuses the show (*Twin Peaks? A Current Affair?*) of transforming the town into a joke. People who have called the crew over to come talk to them, the moment filming starts, go completely deer-in-the-headlights frozen.

Upon seeing the film crew, a workman carrying a chainsaw runs straight down, at a forty-five-degree angle, the wooden roof he's repairing, jumps onto the bed of his truck, and bounces over to the camera crew. Again, the moment filming starts, he just keeps grinning and can say absolutely nothing at all to what are by now to my ears all the usual questions: how many people have you mowed down with that thing this week, etc. Once the interview is over, he runs after the crew and says that he might not be a good actor—he's been asked to say, "Until *next* time, America," then fire up his chainsaw—but that he's a hell of a good carpenter; the chain saw feels like it's attached to his hand. He's explaining, in effect, why he's flunked the screen test: the chainsaw rather than the camera is his weapon. Still, he wants to know when the show will be on.

Then Watkiss turns and asks whether he hasn't seen my photograph somewhere before—in the post office perhaps? Weakly I mumble something about the FBI's Most Wanted list. Then he asks how many people I've murdered this month. I try to play along by saying, "Twenty-seven." "Does your mother know about this?" he asks, and although a few minutes later I'm able to torture myself by thinking up mildly witty repartee, at the time all I'm aware of are the pincer movements of the cameraman and the soundman and how I'm not talking to Watkiss but to Watkiss in terms of the camera and the way the camera reads him as a perfect and unreal absence and me as a flawed and real presence. I finally say, "I'm not going to do this anymore; turn off the camera."

Ten seconds after they relent, I'm instantaneously and immensely glib about the power of the camera to distort and judge and serve as a kind of actor in a triangulated drama. I even manage to launch into an exceedingly obvious diatribe against the shoddy sensationalism of *A Current Affair*, but nothing I say carries any weight the rest of the afternoon, because it's so obvious that for an endless moment I've fallen prey to the awesome power of something toward which I pretend absolute irony: I wanted the camera to find in me, and love me for, qualities that I don't and couldn't possibly possess. The crew moves on to the next person, and I brandish my quaint pencil and notepad as earnestly as the builder had his chain saw.

The Nimbus of His Fame
Makes a Nullity of Us All

Laura Elliott/Seattle Times

Danita Fitch and G. R. Heryford were fired from Red Robin after they tried to persuade a pregnant customer not to have a daiquiri because alcohol could damage the fetus.

Robert DeGiulio/Seattle Post-Intelligencer (The New York Times)

G. R. Heryford and Danita Fitch, dismissed from their jobs at the Red Robin restaurant near Seattle

Rich Frishman (Newsweek)

Local heroes: *Fired cocktail waiters in Seattle*

AP/Wide World Photos

"I wanted to be famous—rich and famous. And I was always dying for people to pay attention to me."
—WOODY HARRELSON[29]

About the Author

Bob Fowler

Jerry Bauer

David Shields graduated, Phi Beta Kappa, from Brown University in 1978 and received his Master of Fine Arts degree from the Iowa Writers' Workshop. He has

David Shields is the author of a previous novel, *Heroes*. His stories and essays have appeared in *The Iowa Review*, *Chicago Review*, *James Joyce Quarterly* and *South*

Tom Collicott

Timothy Greenfield-Sanders

David Shields graduated from Brown University and the Iowa Writers' Workshop. His previous books are the novels *Dead Languages* and *Heroes*. He has received

"Most successful art is glamorous. Glamour is precisely the quality of being able to make people take what you say at face value."
—DAVID SALLE[30]

Why We Live at the Movies

At first my sunglasses are too dark. They also seem to have an odd tint to them. It doesn't take long, though, before I become accustomed to the discoloration and the shade. The reds and blues still look red and blue. I find that if I wear the sunglasses long enough I can't feel them anymore. It's as if they aren't even there. Everyone says they're better for my eyes, but the oddest thing happens when I take them off: I feel like I suddenly can't see.

Desire

Women wear glasses on chains, like metal dogs on a leash. They whip them around in the air like a lasso. They bite the earpiece of the temple, than which simply nothing is more suggestive. They lay their glasses down on the table, allowing the whole world to go fuzzy on them, while they rub their eyes. They crawl around on the floor, looking for their glasses, which they can't find because they're not wearing their glasses. They find their glasses and hug you in a frenzy of unblurry relief. They clean their glasses with your T-shirt. They read in bed. They place their glasses on top of their head like deep-sea divers emerging from the deep sea. They push them halfway down their nose so they can neither see you nor not see you, so you can neither see them nor not see them. They remove their glasses, exposing the little red indentation across the bridge of their nose. They smash their glasses while making love to you. They tuck their glasses carefully in a case, like putting a baby to bed.

A woman recently riding the crosstown bus struck me as extremely beautiful, if in a rather traditional, all-American way; without glasses, she would have been a statue, a mannequin, a doll, a cartoon: her beauty would have been too too. Her simple red tortoiseshells eroticized her to an almost intolerable degree. They drew me in and stood me off. They said, "You can look at me all you want, but you can't see me in public. You have no idea what I look like or am like. You have no idea how interesting things get when I take these off. I'm so sexy I need to wear these as a buffer."

The way her glasses worked against her beauty was exactly what made her more beautiful: more human. Glasses insist upon the constant simultaneity of body and mind; the beauty of a woman's face is deepened and complicated by the antiglamour scholasticism of her eyewear. Superman without Clark Kent would be perfect, completely unconvincing, boring.

Glasses have the spectacular virtue of suggesting that there is everything left to imagine: only someone in special circumstances will see the veil removed, the gate opened, the cage unlocked—her naked eyes. Only I get to see her without her glasses; only I get to see the beauty behind the barrier. Glasses make completely explicit the relationship between eyes and I, between love and trust. Glasses, mask of masks, allude to the difference between how a person appears in public and how the same person might perform in private, and thus suggest the bedroom. The arrogance implied in believing that one's beauty can afford to be concealed is entrancing. By contrast, people not wearing glasses sometimes seem preposterously accessible, uncomplicated, unmysterious, trampy.

What's so sexy about glasses is that they block the male gaze and return it redoubled; they transform the woman from viewed to viewer, from looked-at to looker. *Men seldom make passes at girls who wear glasses*—Dorothy Parker's aphorism tells us much more about her particular brand of self-loathing than it does about eyewear. "Smell me, touch me, but don't look at me": needless to say, this is a tantalizing message to send.

When a woman wears glasses, she is—to me, anyway—displaying her woundedness. (In the wild, a wounded animal doesn't get courted.) She seems both very vulnerable—I could remove her glasses, causing her to be disoriented—and very brave—choosing not to conceal her defect in the most vital of the five senses. One sense is diminished; another sense—touch? taste?—must, in order to compensate, be particularly acute.

In high school I read Philip Roth's *Goodbye, Columbus*. The book opens like this: "The first time I saw Brenda she asked me to hold her glasses. Then she stepped out to the edge of the diving board and looked foggily into the pool; it could have been drained, myopic Brenda would never have known it. She dove beautifully, and a moment later she was swimming back to the side of the pool, her head of short-clipped auburn hair held up, straight ahead of her, as though it were a rose on a long stem. She glided to the edge and then was beside me. 'Thank you,' she said, her eyes watery though not from the water. She extended a hand for her glasses but did not put them on until she turned and headed away. I watched her move off. Her hands suddenly appeared behind her. She caught the bottom of her suit between thumb and index finger and flicked what flesh had been showing back where it belonged. My blood jumped."[31] Immediately I was deep into Brenda.

"Now what can you do?" I once asked a lover who, in bed, had just removed her glasses and who without glasses was legally blind. I thought I meant "How well can you function without your glasses?" but my question clearly implied another question—concerning mattress acrobatics. I wanted her to put her glasses back on so I could tear them off.

Is anything more unnerving than to be asked, in the middle of a lovers' quarrel, "Why won't you look at me?" The eyes, as the Renaissance never gets tired of telling us, are the windows of the soul. What glasses say is: "My soul is not so easily accessible."

The terms for frame parts are about the distance between me and you, between here and there—rim, bridge, hinge, shield. Some temple parts: bend, shaft, and, um, butt portion. Is everyone aroused by looking at diagrams of glasses, or is that only me? I love how the long thin temples screw into round liquescent lenses. In the interest of full disclosure: absolutely nothing could possibly be more erotic to me than the subservient-yet-unreachable paradox embodied by a woman performing fellatio while wearing glasses.

I must acknowledge that some things about glasses just don't work. All sunglasses, for instance, strive so strenuously to be mysterious that they have zero effect on me. So, too, the cat's-eye, which is much too obvious in its female = feline, CatWoman = bitch-goddess equations. Movie stars at the Academy Awards wearing horn-rims in order to read the TelePrompTer do not suddenly seem deeper and more widely read. Pornographic photos—intended to excite the bookish gentleman—in which glasses are perched on the tip of the model's nose as a totally alien accessory are not very exciting. Glasses can't be a self-consciously sexy accoutrement; the joke can't be explained; the contradiction can't be resolved in favor of overtness: glasses are sexy precisely to the degree that a woman's sexiness appears to emerge despite her attempt to hide it.

An ex-girlfriend needed glasses only to drive at night and read subtitles in movie theaters. As often as possible, I would tell her I wasn't sure I knew the way home—would she mind driving? As often as possible, I suggested that we sign up for, say, the Fellini retrospective at the Grand Illusion.

And yet, finally, no one, as I've learned all too well, wants to hear: "I love how you look in your glasses; I think you look even better with them on." The sexiest thing about glasses is that they come off. The sexiest thing about glasses is that the first time you kiss, she lets you take them off and then she blinks once, trying to focus.

Where We Live and What We Live For

She does not wave to the crowd, nor does she nod. She steps out of the limousine far enough for the door to be shut behind her, and then she turns her face like a shield, and on it is written, "This is what you came to see." And then she goes in. I saw Joan Crawford with the naked eye and she was *radioactive* with belief in herself. My image was *burned* on the wall behind me. Quite extraordinary. *Blazing.*

—QUENTIN CRISP

I played Two Truths and a Lie with a man waiting with me for the airport shuttle; one of his truths was that he'd been the Gerber baby.

My cousins used to live in the same building at Central Park West and Ninety-third as did William Hurt and Marlee Matlin, whom I once stood next to in an elevator going down.

The first question a friend of mine (a house painter who was married for a time to Clare Booth Luce's granddaughter) would always ask people who lived at an expensive New York address was: "Who's in your building?"

I stood in line behind Linda Hunt at a cleaner's in the Village, sat next to Ed Koch at the premiere of *Zelig*.

I watched Teri Garr shop, solemnly, for swimwear at Bloomingdale's.

I walked past Fran Lebowitz on Fifth Avenue and asked her how her well-known work-in-progress was coming along.

On a sweaty summer day I bumped into Tom Wolfe on Central Park South; he looked like a vanilla ice cream cone, melting.

My ophthalmologist had a drawing by John Updike on the wall.

I sat in a doctor's waiting room, flipping through magazines with Alfred Kazin.

The soda jerk, mixing my milkshake, tossed canisters in the air and behind his back exactly the same way Tom Cruise did when preparing drinks in the just-released *Cocktail.*

An ex-girlfriend's friend's father (who told every new inamorata that she had "unlocked his cock") was shrink to the stars and invited me to a party in Malibu Colony at which I dined on the same back porch with but not really in very close proximity to Steve Martin, Dustin Hoffman, Dinah Shore, Walter Matthau, Jack Lemmon, and Beethoven's Fifth Symphony playing in the background. Walter Matthau said he'd never seen his wife without her makeup.

A former student of mine went out with Elizabeth Montgomery's son.

A friend of a friend showed up at Arnold Schwarzenegger's hotel room for a date, and Arnold greeted her in his underwear.

I rented an apartment in Echo Park that was once inhabited by Tom Mix.

I watched Ted Danson get into his car outside a 7-11 in Santa Monica at Wilshire and Fifth, and was struck by his desire to initiate and sustain rather than avoid eye contact with putative fans.

Ditto David Susskind, when I stood in a stuck hotel elevator with him for a couple of minutes.

Ditto Tony Kubek, when I sat next to him on a bumpy plane ride from Chicago to San Francisco.

For a brief time I lived next door to Berke Breathed in Iowa City; he'd go out with people to a Chinese restaurant and tell them how many newspapers now carried his comic strip.

When I was a kid, my family and I had dinner in Georgetown at Daniel Schorr's—my mother's friend's husband—house and watched him watch the *CBS Evening News* and bemoan, at extraordinary length, the diminution of his report.

At a Thai restaurant in Seattle I sat catty-corner from Bill Gates and overheard him say something something something something "compared to my personal wealth."

Twice I'm pretty sure I've seen Gary Larson walking around Seattle.

When Kurt Cobain committed suicide, I found myself mentioning several times a day that I knew someone who knew someone who claimed to be his supplier.

In *Swimming to Cambodia*, Spalding Gray says, "The Marines were thrilled to have real actors on the base. One of the Marine guards who had escorted us onto the helicopter got a Polaroid picture of the scene from Continuity and asked us, 'Would you please sign this picture for me? I want to send it to my folks in North Carolina. Because if I never do anything else in my life, at least I can say I have done this.'"[32]

Where We Live and
What We Live For

My favorite joke goes:

This guy Mario says to his friend Vito, "You know, Vito, I know everybody in the world there is to know."

Vito says, "Oh, give me a break."

"I do. Just try me."

"I'll bet you a thousand bucks that you don't know, oh, Robert De Niro."

"Oh, Bobby," Mario says. "Bobby and I went to high school together. Back in New York. We used to go drinking all the time."

They fly to New York. TriBeCa—a loft. They knock on De Niro's door. He's deep in preparation for his next role.

"Oh, Mario," De Niro says. "How good to see you. Bourbon and water?"

"You know," Vito says to Mario, "you said you knew everyone in the world there was to know, but I can't believe you know Robert De Niro."

"I told you I knew everyone in the world there was to know," Mario says.

"I'll bet you two thousand dollars that you don't know the queen of England," Vito says.

"Oh, the queen and I, old Queenie, we were equestrians together. We used to wash the horses down."

So they fly to Buckingham Palace and get there right at the changing of the guard. Pomp and circumstance. Who answers the door but the Queen herself!

"Oh, Mario," she says, "so good to see you."

Mario and Vito follow her into the palace.

Vito says, "Mario, when you told me that you knew everyone in the world there was to know, I couldn't believe you. But now I see that you know Robert De Niro and the queen of England. Still, I'll bet you five thousand dollars that you don't know the Pope."

"Oh, John Paul," Mario says. "Ol' Popesie Opesie. We're close friends, very close friends. The pontiff and I took our secret vows together. Man, did he love those wafers."

They fly to Vatican City. It's Easter Sunday. Long throngs of ecstatic Catholics are awaiting the Pope's arrival.

"Vito," Mario says, "I have to tell the Pope that I'm here, so you stand here between these two nuns and you'll be just fine."

Mario goes running up the steps to the Pope's apartment, and pretty soon, on the balcony of the Vatican, the Pope and Mario appear arm in arm, waving to the crowd, blessing the crowd one and all.

Mario looks down and sees Vito faint.

"Excuse me, Pontiff," Mario says, "I'm terribly sorry, but I have to go check and see what's the matter with my friend Vito."

So he goes out and runs down the steps and pushes past the cardinals—the crowd parts like the Red Sea—and he gets through and finds Vito and he goes, "Vito, what's the matter with you? Are you all right?"

And Vito kind of wakes up in a daze and says, "Mario, when you told me you knew everyone there was to know in this world, I couldn't believe it, but when these two nuns pointed up and said, 'Who's that guy with Mario?' . . ."

Where We Live and
What We Live For

A State of Mind

This must be our one true national sport—rubbing shoulders with the great, the near-great, the ingrate. In the middle of its first full season on the air, Matt Nodella and Tom Leetch, the producer and production manager for *Northern Exposure*, speak to the Washington Film and Video Association at Triples, a restaurant in Seattle. Nodella is young and tall, wears sneakers, has a neatly trimmed moustache, and says, with a little too much enthusiasm, a little too much sincerity, "Filmmaking is a lot of fun. It can be exciting. It can be invigorating." Leetch, on the other hand, mentions something about brushing his teeth with Red Hook ale.

Northern Exposure is, according to Nodella, "a show which from its inception was a little different: something to shake up this business." I don't understand what's so revolutionary about the show until Nodella explains that summer series (*Northern Exposure* originally broadcast eight episodes the previous summer) are a real anomaly.

Leetch emphasizes that "this is a more sophisticated time for TV. People are expecting more. With the tube eating up so many hours, there's a lot of decentralization going on, a scattering toward regional centers, to give the public a better look." Nodella found the look he wanted—an Alaskan town—in Roslyn, eighty miles east of Seattle.

Alaska didn't have the "crew requirements, the people requirements." Besides, Alaska is, according to Nodella, a "state of mind."

Someone asks Leetch whether this spring *Northern Exposure* will be paying crew overtime after twelve hours, and he says, "Didn't we talk to him before?"

Asked whether he's experienced any frustrations with working here, Leetch says, "In some areas, people could have had a little more experience." Then he looks around. "Chuck—present company excluded."

"Any other frustrations?" the moderator asks him.

Leetch says he wishes Chapman Cranes and Honey Wagons were available in Seattle, and adds: "You bring in a smattering of people who have been spoiled with all these toys, these goodies, and it's hard."

A number of people urge Nodella to consider having postproduction services performed in Seattle rather than Los Angeles. He responds by saying that "you would need to have executive producers who wouldn't mind living here."

"We could save you a day," someone says.

"I know you do very capable posting," Nodella says, "but the executive producers—"

"There are more D-1 [digital editing] houses here than anywhere in the world."

"It isn't my decision," he says, somewhat exasperated.

"I'm sure that we didn't mean this to be confrontational," the moderator says.

"The people here are wonderful," Nodella concludes. "Washington is a beautiful state: the rich colors, the variety of locations, the trees on the hillsides. It's unique in its greenness; that's something that you should definitely promote."

A Couple of Head Shots

Until the show's demise in the spring of '95, Elaine Miles played the character of Marilyn, Dr. Fleischman's Native American assistant. She had never acted before. Her mother heard that the producers were looking for someone "short and stout, with a Native American Indian look." Miles decided to tag along so she could "sit around and look at all the movie stars," but then she was asked to read. "I read sides [her portion of the script], they videoed me, and then they asked me to do it again and I thought I must have done something wrong." She got the part on a Monday and started shooting on Tuesday.

Miles is enrolled on the Umatilla reservation, where she's a member of the Cayuse / Nez Perce tribe. Born in Pendleton, Oregon, she moved to Seattle when her father got a job as a machinist at Boeing. She graduated from Renton High School. As she says, "Part of me is Native American Indian; part of me isn't." Her conversation flows wildly and seamlessly from discussion of powwow dancing and the Lewiston roundup to extended contemplation of a purchase of a "GMC pickup, cab-and-a-half, short bed, four-wheel drive, AM/FM cassette stereo, air conditioning, tinted windows. A Porsche is a prissy car: touch it and it's a wreck."

She's more interesting in person than in her "wooden Indian" role on the show—in Miles's own words, "a kickback character with ESP"—so I ask her to talk about the only thing I ever seem to care about: the difference between life lived and filmed.

"I don't like me, I don't like Marilyn, wearing her hair in braids," she says. "Indians in Alaska have perms and beauty parlors and stuff. That makes me mad." She points out the mismatched pink pants and turquoise shirt she's wearing and says, "I hope they don't make me wear these clothes again this year. I don't think they will. I'm not so inexperienced this year."

Miles says that she's directed to speak much more slowly than she would ordinarily, and she gives an example from the show's pilot. At one point, she tells Dr. Fleischman that a man is continuing to work out his differences with his wife, who has shot him. Miles says that she wanted to say the line the way she ordinarily would—"They're still talkin'; I'll stitch 'im up"—but that she was told to speak with exaggerated enunciation: "They're still tawk-ing. I'll stitch him up." She was directed to stretch out the word "stitch" to sound childlike and quaint: a foreigner's formal English.

Miles acknowledges that last summer, when *Northern Exposure* was first being broadcast and she traveled to powwow dances, she "got quite a lot of criticism" from people in her own tribe and other tribes for portraying a stereotype. She says she lost a lot of friends, attributing their reaction to envy over her money and fame. "Excuse me," she says, "but they pissed me off." In Albuquerque, on the other hand, a couple of Navajo cowboys kept "shaggin' on" her, following her around wherever she went until they finally went up to her and asked if she was Marilyn on *Northern Exposure*. When she said she was, they told her how much they liked her on the show and how happy they were to discover that she was, in fact, Native American.

"I gave 'em a couple of head shots," she says.

One-Legged Tap Dancer

On *Northern Exposure*, Barry Corbin—who played gruff, macho, irascible types in such films as *Urban Cowboy*, *War Games*, and *Any Which Way You Can*—played Maurice Minnifield, an ex-astronaut and the overbearing president of the small town's Chamber of Commerce. I have just caught him on television in a Birds Eye commercial, in which he plays a gruff, macho, irascible type, and so when I interview him immediately after interviewing Miles, my first question isn't oblique: how does he feel playing the same kind of character over and over has affected his own personality?

He snaps out of character—gruff, macho, irascible—into a more meditative mode and is interesting and forthcoming on the subject; I'm the naïf for assuming typecasting was fate. "Well, we all invent ourselves," he says by way of preface, and I feel the cartoonish nature of the image I strive to project: ironical whatever. "Most people in their youth want to grab it all, but as you get older, you gain a better sense of who you are, you begin to know what means the most to yourself, and you shed the things that don't. It's an annealing process; you simplify your life. In real life, I've become more and more the rustic character I tend to play in films and television and less and less the New York stage actor I was a long time ago. I'm very interested in horses now. I go in to read for a part and I wear a vested suit, say, but with a western belt buckle."

Corbin mentions that he received many angry letters from disgruntled fans who saw him play, in *The Thorn Birds*, a more refined character than he usually plays. "They want you to *be* that guy," he says, meaning the gruff, macho, irascible type. "The actor Ben Johnson—"

"Ben Kingsley?"

"No, Ben Johnson. *The Last Picture Show*?"

"I love that movie."

"I did a charity rodeo with him and he'd sign autographs without getting off his horse. You redevelop your consciousness. You stay in character. You don't become part of their [the fans'] problem."

He claims that most film actors get typecast after a while and aren't allowed or encouraged to explore their full range. Clark Gable. Humphrey Bogart. Jack Nicholson.

"Why is that?" I ask, though I think I know.

"Because if the movies need a one-legged tap dancer, they can afford to find one. Anybody can create one image. Anybody can write one book," he says. "We're all trapped by ourselves, by our own skins."

I ask him why he thinks people ask movie stars for autographs, and he says, "American Indians have this belief that if you touch your enemy his strength gets transferred to you. It's very primitive: a deranged fan must feel like he's taking your essence."

Corbin finishes up with me by emphasizing the ephemeral nature of film as an art form—"Ninety-nine percent of the movies in a video store: what possible difference could they make to anyone a couple years, a couple months, from now?"—and apotheosizing Literature, mentioning some plays that he has written and that have been produced in New York and Los Angeles, expressing a couple of times his hope of one day playing Lear on Broadway. *Lear?* I think, and only very much later does the possibility occur to me that the moment he met me he recognized my type and instantly changed masks.

Life Is Elsewhere
A Rube's Lament

New York City, increasingly, is used by its resident publicists as a kind of club, with which to beat other regions into prone position. Every actress who has ever so much as sublet a studio apartment in midtown is said to possess something called an "edge": "She has an exceptional beauty, but at the same time her New York background gives her an edge."[33] "California is O.K., but it just isn't me. There's a certain edge that's lacking with a lot of people who, even if they've had it, lose it if they've been out there too long."[34] "Perhaps Ms. Didion brings too much California comfort to her observations of New York. The flip side is that her observations of California have a nice New York edge."[35]

The West Coast in general and California in particular are understood to have as their most noteworthy characteristic the fact that they're not New York: "I spend one week a month out there. That's enough. There's too much sun. The weather is too nice. It makes you too complacent."[36] New York and the East are tough; California and the West are easy: "The Knicks are handicapped by not having the element of surprise or intimidation. The two teams brawled the last time they played in Phoenix, so the fans and the Suns will be ready for the Knicks. There will not be any label of a 'soft' Western team being pushed around by the tough guys from the snow-and-rust belt."[37] "The wisdom among NBA experts is that Eastern conference teams are superior to those in the West because they can play defense."[38] "As far as I'm concerned, the real basketball games are on the East Coast."[39]

A "recurring fantasy" of the editor of the *New Republic* "is one day to quit everything, disappear to Seattle, buy a Starbucks franchise, and generally aim for an idea-less existence."[40] ("New York doesn't need coffee: it is coffee.")[41] A dance critic, coming from New York to Seattle to see the Pacific Northwest Ballet's production of Stravinsky's *Agon*, admires the performance but finds it doesn't work for her because "outside lay the bay on one side, the hills on the other, much too beautiful."[42] A *Times*man takes a summer bike trip cross-country to Oregon in order to report back: "One distinction of this corner of the world is when you tell residents they live in the middle of nowhere, they agree with you."[43]

Descriptions of individuals and events segue, apropos of absolutely nothing, into salutes to "New Yorkers": "[Phil] Jackson [twenty years ago a player for the New York Knicks] was so curious, so alive, so real, so 60's, that he became an icon to many of us who identified, however vaguely, with the counterculture. And what a competitor. What a tough, annoying, persistent sixth man. What a New Yorker."[44] "But what's routine on the streets of New York doesn't work on the runways at LAX. Those paying passengers on flights that were forced to circle overhead while the President had his locks shorn aboard Air Force One are unlikely to be so forgiving as hardened New Yorkers."[45]

For New York is "the city where distractions never sleep,"[46] "a hometown of unforgiving realities."[47] It's a city that's calculated to diminish you."[48] "No one is capable of functioning well, let alone being content, in the cauldron that is New York."[49] And yet—or, rather, and so—"New York is the last true city."[50] "I couldn't live anywhere else."[51] "Living anywhere else is unimaginable."[52] "There is nowhere else to live."[53] "Let's pretend for a moment that we're on the moon, O.K., and we're looking down on the Earth, the big globe. And some person from the moon comes up and asks you to pick out the center of the globe, 'cause you can see it from up there, you know. New York is the center of the world."[54]

All athletic endeavor is thought to be best appreciated as a game of geographical chicken. Bobby Bonilla grew up in the South Bronx, played professional baseball for the Pittsburgh Pirates, and was traded to the New York Mets, for whom he's been an expensive disappointment. Therefore, "Bonilla cannot handle New York."[55] "And now, Bonilla seems to many to be intent on proving he is smarter than the rest of New York or tougher than it—or both."[56] "Bonilla just may not be cool enough to have a long career in New York.

Nothing against him. This is a hard town these days, and only the strong survive. New York is not for everybody. Not even locals. It may not be right for Bobby Bo."[57] So he was traded to Baltimore.

Although they had the home-court advantage, in 1993 the New York Knicks lost the series for the Eastern Conference championship to the Chicago Bulls, four games to two: Assaulted by intolerance from the East River to the Hudson, the Bulls hoped to maintain a mental edge through a determined patience and a better understanding of their working environment. Patience. In New York. Imagine that."[58] The Chicago Bulls won, but they're not real New Yorkers: they're not impatient. "The Knicks knew better than to count on home-court advantage this year because New York fans don't have the single-minded xenophobia of the other towns": The Knicks lost because their fans are too sophisticated; they're real New Yorkers.[59]

"My house, and most houses out here on the West Coast, aren't 'real'":[60] it's almost impossible for me to shake this feeling of inauthenticity, almost impossible to overemphasize the degree to which growing up in the West felt like a shadow life, as if somehow it didn't really matter, didn't quite count. From my nostalgic father, a New York native; every magazine atop the toilet tank; and the air-mailed New York Times sitting on the welcome mat every day when I got home from school—all I heard or read about was the idea of elsewhere. What is it, anyway, about black-and-white ceramic tile bathroom floors, white wooden window sills, coat racks in hallways, and roof terraces with views of the Hudson River that confers meaning upon existence? Every Manhattan street address is still, for me, a quick haiku of glamour.

And yet when, the summer of 1969, our family made our first trip "back east" and stayed with my aunt on Riverside Drive, I was positively tremulous with anticipation but unwilling to test the concept against reality, so I spent virtually the entire time locked in my room, watching Mets and Yankees games. When, as an adult, I lived for a few years on West Eighty-ninth Street, I was so excruciatingly self-conscious about the fact that I was living a life I'd fantasized about since I was six years old that I would often literally turn around to look for cameramen filming what felt like someone else's corny movie. I'd thought about the place so much I'd used it up as a livable idea. New York is: what would my life be if it weren't my life?[61]

Almost Famous

On Howard Stern's radio show on WXRK in New York (and on his cable-television show), "Stuttering John" Melendez—whose favorite fictional character is Cornelius, King of the Apes, whom he resembles and whom he imitates whenever the opportunity arises—asks, tries to ask, Barbara Eden what she sleeps in; Magic Johnson why *baseball* players are so horny; Valerie Harper whether she has breast implants and whether her husband spanks her; Gennifer Flowers whether then-Governor Clinton used a condom; Joey Adams when the last time was he had a solid bowel movement; Chastity Bono if she's ever French-kissed Cher; Liz Smith why she's such a fat cow; Walter Mondale whether he ever worried that Geraldine Ferraro would get cramps in office; Morton Downey Jr. if his wife would dance topless to save him from poverty; Liza Minelli why gay guys dig her mom so much; Warren Beatty what's bigger—the Oscar or his penis.[62]

The questions with which Melendez discomfits celebrities are always sexual, which makes sense: stuttering always seems—to me, anyway—so similar to sexual tension. Melendez says that as a stuttering adolescent, "I had no problem asking other kids if they had hair down there yet. Nobody wanted to talk about it." "The hardest [interview] was Fred Gwynne. I had to promise this girl, this beautiful publicist, that I wouldn't ask him anything about *The Munsters*. I said, 'Hey, don't worry, this is gonna be a piece about his work in the theater,' and she's right next to me, right, when I ask him if he signs his pictures 'Fred Gwynne' or 'Herman Munster.' She's there and you could see her just . . . That's why I stutter so much."[63] "It's like picking up a girl. You've got to go up and ask her out, but it's the most uncomfortable thing."[64] "When I used to try and pick up a girl I would have to turn my head."

Melendez's stutter gets worse whenever the celebrity, stalling for time, asks him to repeat the question, but it's when he's speaking to Stern—before or after the celebrity interviews—that Melendez's voice and face lose all claim to behavioral integrity, for Stern, nicely named, is a merciless sadist:

STERN: What happens if the show goes off the air or somethin' happens to me—what do you do? Seriously, what would you do?

MELENDEZ: Well, b-b-b-by then I hope to have a record contract.

STERN: Let's say a record contract is a tough thing to get, okay? You'll admit that. As much talent as you have, as much natural talent as you have, let's say that never happens. And it looks like it never is gonna happen. You're twenty-six and you're on television. I mean, I haven't seen anybody give you a record contract. What do you do if something happens to me?

MELENDEZ: Cry.

STERN: No, really—what do you do? What is your career path in that case?

MELENDEZ: I don't know, I haven't really given it much, uh-uh-uh-uh, given it too much thought. Maybe I'll take up acting.

STERN: But that's another career. In other words, you have to have, you know, you have to have something to fall back on.

MELENDEZ: I want to be, I want to be in the entertainment industry, you know.

STERN: Right.

MELENDEZ: That's what I've always wanted to do, so—

STERN: All right, so you're in it. Okay, I understand your point. Well, okay.

MELENDEZ: I mean, what is anyone gonna do?

ROBIN QUIVERS [Stern's sidekick]: I like that; he doesn't even think past today.

STERN: Well, you know, they say, if you're going to be successful, don't think past today. That's what all the experts say. I took a lot of courses in this and I know.... You know, he wants to be in show business and the only job he's really qualified for in show business is to sweep up elephant doody at the circus.

MELENDEZ: Could I ask you a question?

STERN: Yes, go ahead.

MELENDEZ: How come, like, you know, I go out, you know, and-and-and-and do this stuff and then, and then, and then, and then, and then you just bring me out and berate me?

STERN: I'm not berating you. I'm concerned about you, like a father to a son. It's a question.

MELENDEZ: All right. I hope that I c-c-c-c-can work with you.

STERN: But what I'm saying—what if it should happen that I am no longer in show business? What, what if I lose my voice to throat cancer?

MELENDEZ: Maybe they'll give me my own show.

STERN: Well, okay, maybe, but you're a friggin' mess.

MELENDEZ: And that's what I'll call it— *The Friggin' Mess Show*.

STERN: That's going to be some show.

Stern calls him "Hero of the Stupid," "Hero of No One," "Stupid Man," "King of the Interns," "world's oldest intern," "stuttering baboon," "oh, you poor man," "you idiot." "What's the matter with you?" "What a turd you are." "There is no show on television that would give an animal like this a job interviewing people for a living. Look at him! What a mess!"[65] Melendez will lock up and Stern will say, "Say it already, you dope"; "Come on, say something"; "If you got something to say, say it quick." Melendez tells Stern that he auditioned for a small role in a Steve Martin movie, and Stern says, "I hope Steve Martin knows hand signals, because this is going to be some movie. This is going to be the longest film ever made. This is going to be a three-hour movie; they're going to have to release it on two separate videotapes." When Melendez's girlfriend appears on the show and Melendez suffers a bad block, Stern repeatedly asks her whether she's embarrassed to be his girlfriend. A man with Tourette's is brought on the show to compete with Melendez for his job.[66] Stern asks Melendez if his jaw ever gets tired, later says, "You know what I just realized? Your jaw reminds me of my mother's sewing machine." "I get a headache from watching you try to talk." "Isn't it fun to wait for the stutter?" Stern asks Quivers. "Seriously, you know, we all feel guilty about it, and let's face it: we all feel terrible that we're watching a guy stutter and we're laughing at him. But you gotta admit you wait for the big stutter, don't you?" Melendez tells Stern, "You know what I think it is? I think—when you point—I think it almost kinda intimidates me." "It intimidates you a little bit? All right, well, I won't point then," Stern says and then points.

One may want to ask of Melendez, as one asks of Bob Balaban: why does he allow himself to be used in this way? Pleading with Liza Minelli for an interview, he promises: "One question, and I swear I'll never talk to you again." After Melendez asks Marlo Thomas whether she and Phil Donahue still get horny for each other, if Marlo ever stuck her finger down her throat, and what the most degrading term for women is, Gloria Steinem interrupts, "You're really hopeless," and Melendez responds, "Why do you say that?" As Susan Sontag says about Michel Leiris's *Manhood: A Journey from Childhood into the Fierce Order of Virility*: "Leiris's attitude is unredeemed by the slightest tinge of self-respect. This lack of esteem or respect for himself is obscene."[67]

Melendez insists that it's not "only funny because I stutter. It's funny 'cause I'm putting these celebrities on the spot."[68] "Celebrities are used to answering the same exact questions over and over again. It's cool to have someone throw them something they're going to have to think about for a second. You see a lot of them break down and become who they really are."[69] "People get all uptight about it. I think it's ridiculous because, I mean, if a celebrity can't, you know, deal with being asked what kind of reading material they read while on the bowl—it's a goofy question, you know, and when these guys get upset about it, you can tell—this is why it's great, it puts them in a true light, out of their character, you know what I mean, out of their usual mode like 'How'd ya get started?'—out of the mode."[70]

If Melendez's stutter expresses the perfect mix of rage and awe we feel before celebrity, the entire operation is an exact mathematical equation of absolute paradox: Melendez doesn't write the questions he asks and often is unaware of the allusions they make to the celebrity's personal problems (thus, even when Melendez is asking the questions, Stern thus keeps him out of the loop); Melendez attempts to treat the celebrities with the same contempt with which Stern treats him, but his stutter—which the *Times* assures us is "under control, for the most part"[71]—is so completely out of control that it immediately undermines his pretense to authoritarian cruelty;[72] Melendez turns into the Jell-O that he's trying to turn them into; using his stutter to make them feel sorry for him and therefore let him talk to them, he exposes the shamelessness of all star-maker machinery, at the same time that he's piercing—with his disrespectful questions—the nimbus around them that they felt certain had made a nullity of us all. If they can't laugh at themselves the way he can—if, as most do, they go grim, get mad, or run away; John Amos, the cookie magnate, asked him, "How did you get a job like this with a speech impediment?"[73]—they expose the gap between their character and their character: they can't even stand toe-to-toe with "Stuttering John," but when they display anything resembling the reservoirs of vulnerability, nerve, and wit that Melendez does, they seem newly, touchingly, weirdly alive. When Melendez asks Reggie Jackson if he ever accidentally farted in the catcher's face, Reggie says, "Sure, and if you hang out long enough, I'll fart in *your* face."[74] Valerie Harper tells Melendez, "I have a dear friend who stuttered, but he communicated right through it and so do you. Isn't it great that you picked this form?"

"Well, I didn't pick it," Melendez says. "I kind of got pushed into it."

"No, I think it's great. What you did is you went into the eye of the storm. That's very courageous."

"Thanks a lot," Melendez says. "C-c-can I get a hug?"

Stuttering

When I was five or six, my sister and I and the other kids on the block would run outside and play *Sea Hunt* the moment the show was over. One of us would be Mike Nelson, "ex-Navy frogman turned underwater troubleshooter," and the rest of us would hide and await rescue.[75] Whenever I was Mike Nelson, I'd always be distracted by and worry endlessly about, say, a broken shoelace or an ant crawling down the back of my neck—off I'd go on a sustained crying jag. I always used to wonder how Lloyd Bridges "battled sharks, octopuses, moray eels, manta rays, alligators, giant sea turtles, Aqua-Lunged badmen, and 'rapture of the deep'" but never got bogged down in minutiae from his own life, why he never appeared to feel lonely.[76]

In elementary school I started stuttering and so I kept a record—dozens of yellow, legal-sized pages—of Robin's "Holy" outbursts, his alliteration and assonance, his fast riffs in sharp contrast to the laconic Batman. Holy Homicide, Batman. Holy Hurricane, Batman. Holy whatever, Batman. One day, oddly (characteristically, self-destructively), I sent my one and only copy of Robin's exclamations to the producers of *Batman*; I thought they might want to have it, for some reason. (I thought it would connect me in powerful, mysterious, and irrevocable ways to the show I spent all week thinking about.) I got back a letter thanking me for my interest, and an autographed photograph of the laconic Batman. I never watched or wanted to watch the show again. I stuttered much worse than usual for a few days, then returned to my usual rate of disfluency.

At twelve, I couldn't not turn friends' names into nicknames based on the names of famous people. Jim Saunders was "Satch," because of Satch Sanders, the Boston Celtics reserve forward to whom Jim bore no resemblance whatsoever. David Morrow became "Agnes Moorehead," or "Aggie," for short. Gary Gogol was "Gookus," after the Philadelphia 76er mediocrity Matt Guokas. Everybody hated me for doing this, but the interesting thing (to me, anyway) was that the nicknames always stuck, often for years and years. We couldn't stand—I couldn't stand—our unamplified little lives.

Childhood, much vaunted, consisted for me mainly of a set of experiments about faith and perception: believing that if I hid my face in my hands, not only could I not see anyone but no one could see me; sitting with my sister in the back of the car, pretending— as they pulled up alongside us—to recognize people in other cars, waving madly at them, getting them to pretend to recognize us and wave back; writing my name, "in cursive," over and over and over again, trying to make my signature look impressive enough to appear at the bottom of checks.

So many movie titles now consist of a two-word phrase such as *Stone Cold* or *Striking Distance* or *Dead Reckoning*: a moribund metaphor literalized until it becomes a violent pun, the point of which is to persuade the viewer that life—which sometimes seems banal, predictable—has hidden reservoirs of excitement and terror.

Robert Capa, Misunderstood

When I write to Mike Watkiss to ask him for a videotape of his report, I include my essay about him. After mailing me the tape, Watkiss calls and leaves this message on my voice mail: "There isn't any question the camera casts a spell over people who come before its unblinking gaze." (The five-minute feature is almost disappointing in its toothless spoofery; he *is* just having some fun with it—no hidden reservoirs of excitement and terror here.)

The Nimbus of Her Fame
Makes a Nullity of Us All

The same day I talk to Watkiss I receive from a friend a fax of a case study in the *New England Journal of Medicine*:

A 45-year-old right-handed woman presented with a four-year history of recurrent episodes of a feeling of pressure in the head, epigastric distress, and mental confusion. These episodes were triggered by the voice of a female cohost on a popular television entertainment program. Two years after the onset of these symptoms, the patient began to have blackout spells that occurred when she was not watching the television program, and she was treated with phenytoin. Her neurologic examination was normal, as was magnetic resonance imaging of the head. Electroencephalography after sleep deprivation was normal. During four subsequent videoelectroencephalographic recording sessions, the patient's complex partial seizures were consistently triggered from the right temporal region by a videotape of the specific television show. Systematic testing revealed that the seizures were precipitated only by the voice of the female cohost and not by visual stimulation, emotional anticipation, or background music; by other programs with similar format; or by other female voices. During a two-year follow-up the patient remained relatively seizure-free by assiduously avoiding the specific program and taking a combination of carbamazepine and divalproex sodium (for blackout spells). She declined behavior therapy aimed at specific voice desensitization."[77]

Where We Live and
What We Live For

The only person ahead of me in line is a red-haired teenager who keeps saying, "Fifty million people. I'm going to be on national TV tomorrow in front of fifty million people." He frequently attends tapings, and he explains to me that the television monitors will be arranged in such a way that you can't see yourself on TV; this is so you won't start waving to yourself.

"Why would you do that?" I ask.

"The familiarity," he explains.

Soon enough, more people start arriving, and virtually everyone is wearing colorful rain gear (a lot of yellows, red, blues, greens) and carrying an umbrella. It isn't raining, but we've been instructed by KOMO to "portray a rain image."

A bearded man behind me turns to his son and says, "Their weekend anchorpeople aren't their top people, but still it would be exciting to see someone familiar, don't you think?" What is this obsession everyone around me has with the filmed familiar? I read in *Newsweek* about a girl who wanted tickets to a New Kids on the Block concert and was quoted as saying: "I just want to breathe the same air that they breathe."[78]

"I told my cousin I'm going to be on national TV tomorrow," the bearded man's daughter tells her friend. "I also told her about that movie they did at my high school."

The bearded man asks me what I'm reading and I show him the cover: *The Unbearable Lightness of Being*.[79] "A novel," I say. "By a writer from Czechoslovakia. It's interesting." He looks at me quizzically, warily. As if to explain that it isn't a subversive tract, I say, "They made it into a movie."

"Oh, yeah, I may have heard of it."

I'm hyperhypochondriachal, and once when I was staying at a hotel in San Francisco, I had the doctor on call come up to my room because I had a *sore throat*. I turned on the 49ers game so we'd have something to talk about and so he wouldn't think I was insane.

It isn't raining, but it's certainly very cloudy, and a chunky little guy comes strutting out the KOMO doors wearing sunglasses. Everyone stares at him until he goes into a convenience store across the street.

We're just outside Chartres, and all any of us care about is the lives of the saints.

We have to pass through a metal detector before we're taken inside into a waiting room and served cookies and coffee. A wall screen is turned, of course, to KOMO and features Saturday morning cartoons.

"No, honey, they're not going to change the channel; it's the only one they get here," a mother explains to her son, who is uninterested in Roseanne Barr as a cartoon character.

"Look at those fries," a kid says to a McDonald's ad.

"Yum, those strawberries look good," his mother says to a Pop Tarts commercial.

A young woman—pretty and a little chilly—hands out address cards for us to fill out.

We all amuse ourselves in different ways during the long wait. Children half-watch the cartoons and eat cookies. Parents drink an extra cup of coffee. I read student stories, and I find myself writing "good" every time one of my creative-writing students mentions popular culture in any way. "Bill got on the bus, lugging his bag of golf clubs, and someone called out, 'Hey, it's Arnold Palmer.'" *Good.* "Nothing ever happened to Lisa's mother that she didn't immediately compare to an episode of 'Days of Our Lives.'" *Good.* The filmed familiar.

The KOMO slogan ("We Are You"), appearing on the screen every fifteen seconds or so as it does, demands contemplation. What does it mean? My unit of one would merge with their oceanic force of many and assuage human loneliness—surely it means that. But what else does it mean?

The man who had escorted us through the metal detector now brings us into the studio. He wears red suspenders and blue socks, is named Dean, and turns out to be the warm-up guy. He explains to us that people from "two other states, Indiana and Boston," are also voting today for one of seven videos to receive the hundred-thousand-dollar first prize. An "all-night editing session," we're informed, will turn today's taping into tomorrow night's half-hour show.

"So how is everybody?" he asks.

The long wait has sapped us, and so we mumble an unenthusiastic "Fine." According to the woman next to me, Dean also does the warm-up for *Northwest Afternoon*, and he apparently has his shows mixed up, because he says, "This is a talk show. This is supposed to be fun, high energy, not"—imitating our blasé response—"'fine.'"

"So how are you?"

This time, people respond more enthusiastically, issuing (the once ubiquitous) Arsenio Hall woofs and circle waves. A poll is taken as to how to pronounce "Arsenio." One woman raises her hand and asks who Arsenio Hall is. Dean asks her whether she has a TV, electricity, hot and cold running water. He urges her to lighten up a little and asks her whether she's going to laugh at all during today's show.

"I'll laugh if it's funny," she says.

The impression she makes is that of a tourist or a dinosaur: a serious, doomed individualist from the old country.

Studio audiences in the four cities—Boston, Indianapolis, Seattle, and Los Angeles—are taping brief exchanges with Bob Saget, the host of *America's Funniest Home Videos*. As Seattle is, the other cities are also rendered as visual cartoons: lobsters, race-car drivers, surfboards. We all laugh at Indianapolis, because they aren't getting the hang of how to vote. When the camera's on you, and you're voting, you're supposed to "hold the voting mechanism very definitely" and, with stylized exaggeration, push the number of the video you want to vote for. Indianapolis, away from the wired world, isn't good at seeing itself as drama.

"Pretend," the Seattle director says nominally to us but more to herself, "that it's 'I move to L.A./I move to New York' kind of voting. Pretend it's monumental."

The script Saget has written for us goes:

"Hi, Seattle, how's the weather today?"

"Rain!"

"How about tomorrow?"

"Rain!"

"What does it do on the plain in Spain?"

"Rain!"

"I think they've got it."

No matter how many times the director who can't decide whether to move to L.A. or New York rehearses it with us, it falls flat, until a bear-like Seattle icon sitting in the front row suggests changing the last "Rain!" to "Rain?" Thus:

"Hi, Seattle, how's the weather today?"

"Rain!"

"How about tomorrow?"

"Rain!"

"What does it do on the plain in Spain?"

"Rain?"

This revision seems brilliant to me, and truly witty, in its implication that Seattleites' imagination fails when it comes to even conceiving of rain anywhere else.

"They loved it!" the director tells us. L.A. approves.

The Seattle producer, the chunky guy who earlier had walked out of KOMO studios into the cloudy morning wearing sunglasses, answers the phone every couple minutes by saying, "Hello, Hollywood, hello." The word comes that, for instance, "L.A. doesn't like bare knees"—a revelation to me—and so the Seattle producer removes the offending girl from the front row. "The kid in the red hair, with the sweatshirt? Don't worry, we'll delete him," Seattle tells Hollywood. I sit right behind this producer, and his abject sycophancy becomes so painful to listen to that I go back to listening to our warm-up guy, Dean, who is learning how to play Nintendo, asking sorority sisters what color lipstick they're wearing ("Natural"), and wondering aloud who wrote the song "Wild Thing."

Bob Saget appears on our monitors. As he's rehearsing with the live audience in front of him and the remote audiences on the satellite uplink, he free-associates in response to no one in particular and apropos of virtually nothing. Some things he says, in approximately this order, are: "Your seat can be used as an air flotation device.... What we want is totally insincere fake laughter; we break you down—that's the secret to my comedy.... This is art; a guy named Art is in charge of it.... I want to work with an adult; I'm half TV host/half day care center.... I can't hear; this is like M.C. Waiting—M.C. Hammer's brother.... What's a satellite? A low-fat saddle.... I used to be funny once.... I'm a minuteman in the video revolution.... My wife and I have two children. Our first was natural childbirth—on a bed of lettuce at the Sizzler. The second, I got to cut the cord, but it was the wrong cord and the lights went out...."

His manner is unmistakably mock vaudevillian—hip, embarrassed, ironic, and depressed in such mercurial and self-canceling combination that his patter, taken in its entirety, amounts to a long (funny) joke about the uselessness and predictability of jokes. It seems admirable, in a way, his capacity to skate instantaneously and incessantly on the light ice of shared reference.[80]

We're finally shown seven videos. The first one is of a girl who cries when she's placed on Santa Claus's lap; in Seattle this receives only two votes. The second video features two very little kids smooching on the floor while a man is trying to give a speech (six votes). Two cats fighting over a bowl of food also receive six votes. A little girl saying a lengthy Thanksgiving prayer—seventeen votes. A dog wrecking a beach tableau by lifting its leg—twenty-five. The winner, both in Seattle, with forty-four votes, and at the other locations, is irresistible footage of a cherubic black kid screaming, rather than merely reciting, his ABCs at a school assembly.

I don't know what it is with me and water, but I find "Boy Sprays Mom" by far the most interesting clip: a mother asks her son to stop spraying water off the sliding patio door; the boy sprays her, and she does a wild dance to get away from the water; she takes the hose away from him and puts it down on the ground; the boy looks terrified and then goes on a major crying jag; the mother laughs one of the world's great laughs and gives him a big hug.

I've taped the episode, and I find myself watching this video over and over. What do I like so much about it? I'm not sure exactly, but it nags at me. "Boy Sprays Mom" finishes fourth.

Problems and Solutions to Problems

The test of a first-rate intelligence is the ability to hold two
opposed ideas in the mind at the same time and still retain the
ability to function.

—F. SCOTT FITZGERALD

DIANE SAWYER: So is Karen Cooper a woman who deserves another
chance to prove she can be a real mother, or should her children
get to choose the parents they want? She lives here, in a halfway house for recovering mental patients in Cedar Rapids. She's
been diagnosed as manic-depressive. There's no cure, but it can
be controlled with medicine. And she is determined that the
children will live with her again.

KAREN COOPER: Why should they be with me? I'm their mother. I
love them. I care about them. I want a chance. I know I've made
a lot of mistakes, but I want a chance. Those are my kids and I
love them. And I don't think anybody can love them like I love
them. I don't care what they say.

SAWYER: But is the Micks' problem that they love them too much?
Do you blame them for loving them too much?

COOPER: Do I blame the Micks for loving them too much? I blame
the Micks for being so selfish and for not—for knowing that the
children loved me to begin with and ignoring that fact.

SAWYER [*voice-over*]: But the children say the Micks never told
them not to love their mother.

COOPER'S DAUGHTER ANNA: No one told us not to love her. Everyone told us, "She's your mother. You're going to live with her. You're going to have a happy time." Mom and Dad did that all the time. And yet Mom and Dad are blamed for taking care of us and providing us a happy home and loving us. Lord, I thank you for letting us stay with Mom and Dad as long as we have, and I hope it'll be longer. I love you, Lord. Amen.

SAWYER [*voice-over*]: When Anna, now twelve, and Amanda, ten, learned that they might have to leave the Micks, they went to a store and tried to buy sleeping pills. They say they really talked about suicide. But the younger children have few, if any, memories of what it was like before. Justin was only three months when his mother gave him up; Sarah was just five and Samantha was three.

[*interviewing*] Do you remember the things that they say happened during that period?

COOPER: No, what?

SAWYER: That they were beaten?

COOPER: That's not true.

SAWYER: Anna says that one time you beat her with a chain.

COOPER: I don't know where she got that.

SAWYER: Never happened?

COOPER: Never. No.

SAWYER: She also says one time she was beaten with a board of some kind?

COOPER: That is true.

SAWYER: That's true?

COOPER: Mm-hmm.

SAWYER: What sort of board? How badly beaten?

COOPER: Well, I was at a girlfriend's house and Anna was trying to make cookies, and the other lady's kids ate all the cookies. Well, Anna just flipped out. You know, I mean, she went into a rage. I looked at the lady and I said, "Do you have a belt?" And she says, "No, use a board. It doesn't leave any marks." I'd never used a board on Anna before, ever. No. Have you ever been hit with a board?

SAWYER: No.

COOPER: It stings.

SAWYER: But you hit her with a board?

COOPER: Yes.

SAWYER: Bruised her?

COOPER: I bruised her leg.

SAWYER: Let me ask you about some of the other things the children have said happened during that time. They say there'd be no food in the house.

COOPER: I don't know about that. I don't remember.

SAWYER: That the clothes were dirty, that the house was dirty.

COOPER: I was washing clothes in the bathtub; the house was dirty. That's true.

SAWYER: Cockroaches and—

COOPER: Yes, we had a lot of cockroaches.

SAWYER: And dogs had gone to the bathroom on the floor.

COOPER: They would do that. That's true.

SAWYER: Anna says, too, that your boyfriend, at least once, threatened her.

COOPER: I wouldn't doubt that.

SAWYER: And beat her.

COOPER: I've never—I didn't know him to beat her. He beat Samantha.

SAWYER: He beat Samantha?

COOPER: Yes, he did.

SAWYER: If you were a child, would you want to go back to it again? Would you want to risk going back to it again?

COOPER: No.

SAWYER: So you understand how they feel?

COOPER: Yes.

SAWYER: Should they be forced to go back to it when they don't know what's ahead? Should they be forced?

COOPER: Forced? Should they give—should they be given an opportunity, as it was planned in the beginning, to let me change? And should I be given a chance?

. . .

SAWYER [*interviewing*]: Did you see the scene on television when they left the Micks'?

COOPER: Yes, I did.

SAWYER: What did you think?

COOPER: It killed me. It hurt.

SAWYER: What hurt?

COOPER: I guess what hurts the most is that they're not mine anymore.

SAWYER: But someone might say, "If you really loved the children, wouldn't you want to see them happy?" And if they are happy with the Micks, wouldn't that be the greater love?

COOPER: Well, I don't know if they weren't happy with me when I was sick and they lived in a house full of cockroaches. They were happy then, too.[81]

Problems and Solutions to Problems

Love your mother. Mothers Against Drunk Drivers. Love is ageless—visit a nursing home resident. Love is caring, sharing, forgiving.

No one is free when others are oppressed. Live simply that others may simply live. Enjoy what you have—hope for what you lack. Hunger hurts. No poverty. Poverty is violence. Fight racism. If you want peace, work for justice. No justice—no peace. No time to hate.

Give peace a chance. Be all you can be—work for peace. Wage peace. Strength through peace. Peace is our only security. Peace is patriotic. Visualize world peace. Peace: back by popular demand. Be your light—be in peace. Think peace. Teach peace. Say your peace. Create peace. Another family for peace. World peace begins at home.

I'm no housewife—I'm a domestic engineer. Every mother is a working woman. The living dead don't do dishes. Wild women don't get the blues. She who laughs, lasts. I can handle any crisis— I have children.

A world of wanted children would make a world of difference. Breed neglect. Pro-child, pro-choice. Pro-choice, pro-family. I'm pro-choice and I vote. Keep your laws off my body. Keep abortions legal and safe. No U.S. intervention in women's wombs. U.S. out of my uterus. Support midwifery. Be a voice for choice. If you can't trust me with a choice, how can you trust me with a child? Catholics for free choice. If men became pregnant, abortion would be a sacrament. If they can send a man to the moon, why can't they send them all? Anti-abortion = anti-sex. Reproductive rights for all women. Abortion: a woman's right to choose. Who decides? If you're against abortion, don't have one. Member of the pro-choice majority. The moral majority is neither.

God is coming and is she pissed! Feminism spoken here. Some women are born leaders—you're following one. Caution: Thelma and Louise on board. Thelma and Louise live. A lady with a gun has more fun. I have PMS and I carry a handgun. You can't beat a woman. Pornography is the theory—rape is the practice. Honk if you believe Anita. Anita told the truth. Listen to women, for a change.

Break the silence. Stop family violence. Another man against violence against women.

Fight AIDS, not people with AIDS. Homophobia is a social disease. Action = Life, Silence = Death. Silence is the voice of complicity. Fight homophobia.

Health care is a right, not a privilege. National health care now.

Friends don't let friends vote Republican. I want to read a bedtime story to Jesse Helms. No God bullies for president. Hate is not a family value.

Invest in America—buy a congressman. Don't steal—the government hates competition. If the people lead, eventually the leaders will follow. The trouble with political jokes is that they get elected. Don't vote.

I love my country yet fear my government. No capital punishment. Why do we kill people who kill people to show that killing people is wrong? Kaos—Revolution—Help destroy Amerika!

Talks, not troops. Stop torture—free Tibet. Free South Africa—end apartheid. Abolish apartheid sanctions now. Death squads and democracy don't mix. Your taxes pay for torture, rape, and murder in Central America. Nicaragua is not our enemy. Stop U.S. attacks—Nicaragua wants peace. ¡Sanctuary *Sí*! El Salvador is Spanish for Vietnam. Stop U.S. intervention in El Salvador.

Do we fear our enemies more than we love our children? War is the real enemy. War is costly—peace is priceless. Say no to war. Honor veterans—no more war. Fight war, not wars. Bread, not bombs. Don't buy war toys. You cannot simultaneously prevent and prepare for war. Cut military spending—rebuild America. Child care, not warfare. It will be a great day when our schools get all the money they need and the Air Force has to hold a bake sale to buy a bomber. No war.

Nuclear war will never determine who is right, only who is left. Stop the arms race, not the human race. The arms race has no winners. Support the freeze. One nuclear bomb can ruin your whole day. Nuclear weapons—may they rust in peace. Boycott GE. Strength through peace. Arms are for hugging. Love is disarming. If we can risk nuclear war, we can risk nuclear disarmament. No rockets.

The earth doesn't belong to us—we belong to the earth. Plant a tree. A city without trees isn't fit for a dog. Save the trees—grow hemp. Log for the future—stop clear-cuts. I'm a friend of the earth. I support plant amnesty. Deforestation is global suicide. Save ancient forests. A healthy forest is no accident. It's a small planet—recycle. Good planets are hard to find—don't blow it. Think globally—recycle locally. Recycle or die. Support organic farmers. Say no to food irradiation. Food—for people, not profit. Nature bats last. Honor necessity. Teach respect for the earth and all living creatures.

Human rights are not special rights. Love animals—don't wear them. Almost missed work today—my pets were too cute. Only elephants should wear ivory. Animals don't wear makeup. No animal testing. Stop crash tests on animals. Catch and return wild trout. Cows kill salmon. Say no to drugs—don't eat farmed fish. Boycott veal—stop factory farming. Save the wolf—boycott Alaska. Thanksgiving is murder on turkeys. Love animals—don't eat them. Friends don't let friends eat meat. Respect life. Help conserve hunters—harvest one today. Beef kills. Heart attacks: God's revenge for eating His animal friends.

Don't let toxic waste make us all endangered species. No offshore oil drilling. Exxon—clean up your act! This vehicle emits carbon dioxide, carbon monoxide, nitrogen oxides, sulphur dioxide, VOCs, benzene, aldehydes, and methane; causes respiratory disease, cancer, smog, and global warming. We're using recycled oil. My other car is a bus. I'd rather be on the train. My other car is a bike. Walk gently on Mother Earth. Listen to the earth. Love Mother Earth. Save the earth.

Give the earth a brake—stop overpopulation. The population problem is everybody's baby. Make love, not babies—ban the population bomb.

Practice random kindness and senseless acts of beauty. Wear a smile—one size fits all. Look for the good and praise it. Speak up for decency. Heal the past, live the present, dream the future. Are you evolved?

One love. One planet, one people ... please. Go jolly: be good, do good, be one. Changing the world, one person at a time. If we do it together, it will work. ALL-R-1.

Wherever you are, be there. KHRPADM. Don't follow me— I'm following my bliss. If you lived here, you'd be home now. Think globally, act locally.

If you're losing the game, change the rules. If you can't change your mind, are you sure you still have one? A mind is like a parachute—it only functions when open.

Weird load. Being weird isn't enough. Just do something. Be part of the solution. Question reality. Question assumptions. Question authority. Subvert the dominant paradigm. Rage against the machine. Reject the illusion. Why just watch TV—why not make it? TV is a drug. Kill your television. The truth you find is within. Resist dogmatic pragmatism. Ignore alien commands. Just visiting this planet. Born Against. Born-again pagan. Acknowledge the pathology of the culture and move on.

Think good thoughts. Think love. Love happens. Magic happens. You never fail until you stop trying. When all else fails, hug your teddy.

The Subject at the Vanishing Point

I attend a march against the Gulf War, and when I confess to my father that I'm constitutionally incapable of participating vivaciously in any sort of group activity, he responds by sending me a series of one-sentence postcards: "Peace in the world or the world in pieces." "Don't stop the world because you want to get off." "It's better to light one candle than to curse the darkness." "If you can move one grain of sand from one spot to another, the world will never be the same." "Lost opportunities never return." "Popular culture, of which you and your generation are so enamored, is *substitute* family, *substitute* community, *substitute* love." "Never again." "It's better to die on your feet than to live on your knees." "We have nothing to fear but fear itself." "Change the world—it needs it." I grew up with these aphorisms, these elegant dicta that were meant to explain everything.

On Friday nights, when my sister and I were in junior high school, my parents would take us to Kepler's, the bookstore of choice for Bay Area radicals; while I was supposed to be tracking down *Soul on Ice* or *Steal This Book!*, I was actually scouring *The Whole Earth Catalogue* and the *Evergreen Review* for pictures of naked ladies.

The summer between my sophomore and junior years of college I worked as a teacher's aide in a remedial summer school in San Francisco. All the students were black and all the teachers except me were black. During the lunch break the teachers screened blax-ploitation films. One afternoon we watched *Mandingo,* a sort of weird southern gothic inversion of the genre. James Mason, the white massa, acted evil; Richard Ward, his slave, plotted freedom; and everybody shouted, "Right on!" Caught up in the action, I, too, shouted, "Right on!" Everyone turned around and stared icily. A line had been crossed, a taboo broken. Though I'd been completely serious, I said, "Just kidding," so we could all get back to watching the movie.

Since I was president of the eighth grade, I was directed, despite my stutter, to address, via the intercom in the principal's office, the entire junior high school on the subject of the eighth grade's appalling behavior at the recent public assembly. I found the assignment so flattering, the power so intoxicating, that I didn't stutter at all. Not once. I don't think I even paused for breath.

I know nothing about planes, but a couple of DC-10s had gone down in recent weeks, so I asked the American Airlines ticket agent, "What kind of plane will we be flying?" "Were you in 'Nam?" she said. Confusion (what does asking what kind of plane we're flying have to do with Vietnam?—only now do I see the connection; she thought I might be carrying explosives) and pride (I'd been mistaken for a soldier) warred in my brain before I said, "Um . . . no."

The summer between high school and college I taped a photograph of each Watergate witness—above his most self-incriminating quotation—on the same wall that I'd once covered with pictures of the

'65 Dodgers. Heroes, villains—it hardly mattered; the subject was where I wanted him: at the vanishing point.

The governor of California once hired me to write a biography of him that would have as its subtitle *Champion of Social Justice*. I quit, or he fired me, when it became increasingly apparent that no one was interested in the champion of social justice except in conjunction with his acerbic son. One day, I was walking with the champion of social justice the few blocks from a restaurant back to his law office in Beverly Hills, when he turned to me and said, "Guess how much it cost me to join the Bel-Air Country Club?" I told him I had no idea. "Fifty thousand dollars," he said.

"I don't buy Coors," I heard someone explain to his roommate in the market. "They're fascists." "They're what?" the roommate said. "They support fascist causes," the man said. "Like what?" the roommate said. "Someone told me what they were," the man said, "but I forget."

Now the only people I like are ambivalent about everything to the point of paralysis.

The Confessions

Why is that? Because the origin of language is ambiguity of feeling. Rousseau's commitment to language signifies his devotion to resolving certain ambiguities in his emotional life, but his decision to rely upon language to discover meaning only drives the paradoxes deeper. His ambition to say everything is analogous to his desire to commit incest: the most extreme, beautiful intimacy combined with a masturbation fantasy of self-love. Rousseau's incest-dream is an attempt to return to a state of innocence, encountering himself in the mirror, self-hating, done up in drag. His compensation for the disaster of his love life is refuge in convoluted language that invalidates the innocence of the love for which he professes to yearn.

Almost Famous

I, too, once wanted to say everything. As a student at Brown in the mid-seventies, I admired my writing teachers, John Hawkes and R. V. Cassill, but both of them were more than thirty years older than I and so I admired them, as father figures, from a distance. I wanted, instead, a teacher who was the older brother I never really had, a hip tutor, a hero to hang out with. Friends at Yale kept telling me about a creative writing teacher named David Milch. He had written speeches for Watergate felon Maurice Stans and songs for the Allman Brothers; he was an alcoholic; he was a compulsive gambler; he had written and discarded three novels of a projected four-book series that R. W. B. Lewis and Robert Penn Warren thought possessed genius; he had been or still was a heroin addict and had served time in a Mexican jail for possession; he was kicked out of Yale Law School for shooting out the lights on a cop car. Who knew how much of it was true? Who cared? I enrolled in Yale's summer session: I wanted him to show me not only how to write but how to live.

Milch looked like he'd never been released from *Rebel without a Cause*: he wore tennis shoes, blue jeans, a pack of Marlboros rolled into the sleeve of his white T-shirt, and a permanent smirk. The only person I've ever known who could convey genuine menace in a classroom, he paced back and forth, chain-smoked, lectured nonstop without notes, rarely allowed anyone to say anything, insisted that we call him "Mr. Milch," addressed us—with pseudo-politeness—as "Mr." or "Miss," and asked questions that somehow were impossible to answer without sounding either feeble-minded or overscrupulous.

John Cheever visited class and Milch asked me whether I thought Farragut, the protagonist of Cheever's new novel, *Falconer*, was "pussy-whipped."

"Define 'pussy-whipped,'" I said.

Joan Didion gave a talk, and afterward Milch made me perform the duty that he had been assigned—selling copies of *A Book of Common Prayer* in the foyer of the auditorium—while he and his sexy fiancée drove away on a motorcycle, reeking of dissipation and glamour.

One student in the class was the son of a famous *New Yorker* writer but had hilariously bad literary instincts. "Whenever you're about to say something," Milch told him in front of everyone, "say the opposite of whatever you're thinking, because whatever you think is always wrong."

No one else's opinion of me and my work had ever seemed so momentous, thrilling, potentially disabling. Although Milch warned us to "never, ever, ever read a review," when we read Sherwood Anderson's story "I Want to Know Why," I looked up what Cleanth Brooks and Robert Penn Warren had said about the story in *Understanding Fiction*, since Milch had studied with both of them and now assisted them in the preparation of revised editions of some of their textbooks. The correct interpretation of "I Want to Know Why" was that it defined loss of innocence as an acceptance of the fact that human beings are not wholly good or wholly evil but a mixture of these qualities.[82] I then rephrased this interpretation so Milch wouldn't recognize the crib, and got praised.

At my first conference with Milch he said, "You're a writer."

I said, "Well, sure, that's why I'm taking the class."

He said, "No: you're a writer."

I bought and ate twelve large chocolate chip cookies at a Greek deli on Elm Street to celebrate.

However, I liked nowhere near as much as Milch did the tortuous circumnavigations of the books he taught: Conrad's *Nostromo*, Faulkner's *Light in August*. One time I pointed out an exceedingly minor inconsistency in *Light in August* about Joe Christmas, and Milch glumly agreed. When I swooned over Henry James's "The Beast in the Jungle," Milch quoted Mark Twain's remark about liking the one James novel he had read but that he wouldn't read another one if you gave him a farm. Milch was a manly man, like Conrad or Faulkner; I, à la James, wasn't.

Both Milch and I liked to write in the new underground wing of the Cross-Campus Library, but I needed the complete isolation of an enclosed cubicle, whereas Milch would work on his stories and plays and screenplays at a table in the center of the room, drinking coffee, overhearing conversation—surrounded by human activity. I allegorized and romanticized this difference: to me, writing was a revenge upon life, upon my life, whereas to Milch writing seemed to be part of life. He was the first intellectual I'd ever met who not only seemed to like life but who reveled in it—who, in Conrad's famous phrase, "to the destructive element submit[ted]."[83] He was—or wanted to appear to be, or succeeded in appearing to be, or succeeded in appearing to me to be (he frequently made sure to take me with him whenever he went to meet his bookie)—that purest contradiction: a macho pedant: a Jewish cowboy.

Although Milch seemed to have picked up a faint southern accent from his association with Brooks and Warren, and his mock fastidious manners evoked for me lapsed southern gentility, he actually grew up in Buffalo, the son of a surgeon. I grew up in San Francisco, the son of Jewish liberal activists. In Milch's class, I wrote elliptical but overwrought stories about this childhood: first kiss, first death, first peace march in Golden Gate Park, etc.—heavy on the water imagery. Milch called these stories "tropisms," which when I looked it up in the dictionary turned out to mean an "involuntary orientation by an organism or one of its parts that involves turning or curving and is a positive or negative response to a source of stimulation."[84] The source of stimulation was my non-fictional family in its perfect righteousness; my response tended toward the negative.

One afternoon, in his austere office in a baroque building, Milch said that I suffered from the "malaise of your [and, of course, his] race": an excessive preoccupation with narrowly moral rather than universally human concerns. As a result, he informed me, I had an insufficiently developed eye. Judaism is a faith rather than a race, but I had recently started wearing glasses and I knew what he meant: I needed to stop judging the world and just see it. *Annie Hall* was the big movie that summer; Milch hated it. He excoriated all my favorite Jewish writers. They were like the boy in "I Want to Know Why"; they hadn't yet learned that human nature was something to accept rather than to protest. The only admirable Jewish American writers were Norman Mailer, who "at least has balls," and Nathanael West, who called Jewish women "bagels." When Milch played softball, he shouted anti-Semitic obscenities from the outfield. All contemporary Jewish American writing amounted, for Milch, to the climactic scene in *Making It*, when Norman Podhoretz has to congratulate himself for being able to enjoy a drink on Paradise Island.[85] Drink, drink, Milch was trying to tell me, drink it all in.[86] Instead, I endlessly repeated back to him his criticisms of me, altering the wording slightly each time so that the criticism didn't sound quite so thoroughgoing and devastating.

"You're classic passive-aggressive," he finally said.

I fiddled with this observation until he threw me out of his office.

Against Milch's advice and without benefit of his recommendation, which he refused to send since he said I needed to get out in the world and live, I went to the Iowa Famous Writers School.

Milch had gone there a dozen years before, so I looked up his master's thesis, a work-in-progress entitled *The Groundlings*, and pored over every line of the two chapters he'd written. The two phrases Milch had used most often in class were "strategy of indirection," which meant it should take the reader forever to figure out what was happening, since life was difficult, and "content tests form," which meant that since life was difficult, it should take the reader forever to figure out what was happening. It took me forever to figure out what was happening in *The Groundlings*, but it had an undeniable narcotic pull, probably because there was so much Milch in it: a protagonist named Torch, ruthless intelligence bordering on the sadistic, extreme emotional candor, incessant obscenity as a mantra of seriousness. He also had what he accused me of having: perfect pitch for how people talked and next to no interest in how the world looked.

The first chapter took place almost entirely in the men's room of an airport in upstate New York. The second chapter was replete, for some reason, with references to Catholic liturgy. Mark and Torch, brothers, spoke to each other in a curious mix of neo-Elizabethan diction ("Speak, knave") and street talk ("Fuck you right in the mouth[,] Torch, I mean it.")[87] It contained two crucial passages for me—I mean for me, personally. Torch tried to talk Mark out of blaming himself for his father's death:

> You've got this compulsion to have some moral relation to every move that's made in this vale of tears.... I mean you made a move. That's all you can do.... Okay, so now you'll go back to ... blaspheming, so everyone will call you a mind-fucker and a shit-bird, and if they don't then you'll call them phonies, because they won't execute divine judgment. That's really a small-change operation[,] Mark. That's really a shitty game to play.... And I mean it's so cheap. It lets you out of every situation, out of letting your moral position be defined by your response to things, by the way you act. You know, by your rules you say if I am of two minds on a problem I am not perfect, and if I am not perfect I am evil, and so you've got your position established without ever having to get involved with the problem itself.[88]

Universally human rather than narrowly moral. And at the end of the first chapter Mark said: "I picked up this guy.... And I fucked his mind! He had just, see, killed his father. By indirection. So I catalyzed it. I got him to see the connection."[89] This was precisely what Milch did for all his students, especially me: catalyzed connections that we knew were there but didn't (but did) want to see, and so we could never stop talking about him.

A few years later, my girlfriend from Iowa, a poet named Karen, and I checked into the Lincoln Hotel in Chicago. Karen's father was a television producer, so we didn't have a TV in our apartment in Iowa City. We were on spring vacation, though. One night a show called *Hill Street Blues* came on. It wasn't just that *Hill Street* seemed more interesting than most things on television; it also seemed instantly familiar, though I'd never watched it before. Bobby Hill bought Renko a prostitute for his birthday, and the prostitute wasn't supposed to tell, but she did. The scene somehow played better than it had any right to, and I told Karen the show reminded me of Milch—its mixture of academic and street idioms, its (I couldn't help it) "strategy of indirection," its very male existential gloom. The credits rolled at the end of the show, listing Milch as story editor, whatever that was. I bounced up and down on the springy bed.

"Take it easy," Karen said. "It's only TV."

I moved with Karen to New York that summer and scoured *Hill Street Blues* every week for the most miniscule revelation about Milch's psychology. The show was full of what were to me recognizable elements from Milch's life, from gambling to loan sharks to heroin to Belker's relationship with his mother. One night that fall, Karen and I sat on the floor of our lilliputian apartment; Milch had been nominated for an Emmy award and so we watched the ceremony on our nineteen-inch black-and-white box. He won for an episode he had written called "Trial by Fury" about Furillo's Cuomo-like conscience. Accepting the award, Milch stood at the podium as if he were back in class, lecturing, and quoted Stanley Kunitz to the effect that "you are all my brothers in the world." Kunitz was one of Karen's favorite poets; she knew the reference was to his famous poem about the Holocaust, "Around Pastor

Bonhoeffer," which contained the question: "*If you permit this evil, what is the good / of the good of your life?*" We looked up "Around Pastor Bonhoeffer." The final section was called "The Extermination Camp":

> Through the half-open door of the hut
> the camp doctor saw him kneeling,
> with his hands quietly folded.
> "I was most deeply moved by the way
> this lovable man prayed,
> so devout and so certain
> that God heard his prayer."
> Round-faced, bespectacled, mild,
> candid with costly grace,
> he walked toward the gallows
> and did not falter.
> Oh but he knew the Hangman!
> Only a few steps more
> and he would enter the arcanum
> where the Master
> would take him by the shoulder,
> as He does at each encounter,
> and turn him round
> to face his brothers in the world.[90]

For anyone ready to "catalyze the connections," false modesty turned rapidly into whiplash judgment.

My first novel was published in the winter of 1984. I sent *Heroes* to Milch, who a year later left a message on my answering machine that he'd liked the book—"a nice novel about a kid growing up," according to Milch, whereas in actuality it's about a diffident Iowa sportswriter obsessed with a brilliant and uncouth college basketball player.

A couple of years later I went to Yaddo, beginning a new book. It wasn't nice, but it was a novel about a kid growing up (a self, stuttering). One afternoon Milch drove into the parking lot with his wife and daughter. He got out of the car and told me to give them the tour. With the money he'd made from *Hill Street*, he'd bought a horse and had come to Saratoga to watch it race. Since I hadn't seen him for ten years, I was astonished, and secretly delighted, that he recognized me immediately. He said that when he'd been here years ago he'd found it "a good place to dry out" but hadn't written a thing, and the only thing he'd looked forward to every day was reading the paper, because "at least it was a little hit of the real world." We walked through the ridiculously medieval main mansion. I pointed out that the founder of Yaddo had made his fortune in the railroad business and later been killed in a train wreck. "That," I said, "is known as poetic ... something or other." Milch laughed. This was funny—to be smart enough to know when to pretend you don't know something. He gave me a phone number to call so we could get together; I called a few times and left messages and he never called back.

The book I had worked on at Yaddo was published in 1989. I sent him a copy, and shortly afterward he left a message on my answering machine, asking me to call him back immediately. When I called, his assistant asked whether *Dead Languages* had been optioned yet, and I thought: yes, yes, sweet revenge, Milch likes the book so much he feels compelled to make it into a movie. He wasn't interested in making it into a movie and never had been. He was the executive producer of a television show called *Capital News* and wanted to know whether I wanted to make four hundred thousand dollars a year writing teleplays. He sent me a cassette of the pilot, to which I knew I was supposed to respond by coming up with new scenarios. But the show was dismal—*Capital News* was like *Hill Street Blues* on Thorazine—and I couldn't come up with anything, so I pretended I didn't understand exactly what it was he was looking for from me and mailed him a lengthy, not to say interminable, critique of the pilot. When he never replied, I called him and was put on hold for the longest time. While waiting, I planned my speech about how I hoped he took my response in the spirit in which it was intended: as *constructive* criticism; how the show had a lot of good moments and plenty of potential and there was nothing about it that couldn't be fixed if—

He put me on the speaker phone, explained that my critique was moot since the pilot was already in the can, dispatched me in thirty seconds, and started talking on another line before I'd even hung up.

What exactly did I seek so earnestly from this mentor / tormentor, this brilliant bully, and why did he so steadfastly refuse to give it? Why did he always tease me by positioning himself close enough to view but just out of my grasp? Antagonizing me, he was also showing me in person what he wanted me to do on the page. "Strategy of indirection": life is difficult: describe the difficulty.

Why We Live at the Movies

Writer A says, "There is no such thing as a famous novelist now, any more than there is such a thing as a famous poet. I use the adjective in the strict sense. According to authority, to be famous is to be much talked about, usually in a favorable way. It is as bleak and inglorious as that. Yet thirty years ago, novels were actually read and discussed by those who did not write them, or, indeed, read them. A *book* could be famous then. Today the public seldom mentions a book, though people will often chatter about the screened versions of unread novels. What, after all, do we most love to talk about? Movies."[91]

Writer-turned-screenwriter B says, "There is one thing that is more powerful than dope, and that's movies. Because even people who don't like dope love movies. Everybody loves movies. All you've got to say is *Sea of Love*, or *Color of Money*, and people look at you. They go weak in the knees. Like, 'Would you call him Al, or would you call him Mr. Pacino?' All of a sudden you're like this bridge standing between them and this dream factory we all grew up on. And we're all dopey about."[92]

Writer C, in conversation, says that Writer D wrote a truly great novel, but too late; by the time Writer D wrote a truly great novel, the time for truly great novels was already over. It simply didn't matter that Writer D had written a truly great novel; in fact, according to Writer C, it shouldn't have been written.[93]

There's no longer any possibility, in other words, of ever reaching, as Writer E once hoped, "a vague spot a little to the east of Kansas, where a countryish teenaged boy could find [Writer E's] books on the library shelves without their jackets, years old, and have them [Writer E's books] speak to him."[94]

Both of my parents were freelance journalists who wanted to write books and never did and so idolized writers. I stuttered and so I, too, worshipped the written word. In junior high and high school I was the editor of the paper.

In college I wanted to be a "New Journalist" until I got in trouble for making stuff up. I started spending long hours in the Marxist bookstore just off campus, reading and eating my lunch bought at McDonald's; I loved slurping coffee milkshakes while reading and rereading Sartre's *The Words*. I closed the library every night for four years; at the end of one particularly productive night, I actually scratched into the concrete wall above my carrel, "I shall dethrone Shakespeare."

Fueled by such ambition, I was a good bet for graduate school, where my first creative-writing teacher said that she wished she were as famous to the world as she was to herself, and my second creative-writing teacher said that if he had it to do over again, he'd have become a screenwriter. A famous actor wanted to meet me before optioning my first novel, so I flew to Toronto, where he was making a movie; he walked around at night and made eye contact with prostitutes until they recognized him, then he'd wink and laugh and inform them that it was cold out, better bundle up.

Why We Live at the Movies

The test of a first-rate intelligence is the ability to hold two
opposed ideas in the mind at the same time and still retain the
ability to function.

—F. SCOTT FITZGERALD

Sometimes the only way to find where you're going is to lose your
way. The road ahead was the only way to leave the pain behind.
Her life began when her world fell apart. When the world turns
upside down, the trick is to come out on top. When you're down
to your last dream, you either live it or lose it. He left behind everything he knew for the only thing he ever wanted. Mary Alice left
the New York rat race to join the human race. A son who's starting
out—a mother who's starting over. Jon really drove his parents
crazy when he was growing up—they're about to return the favor.
For country music star Buddy Parks, the shortest distance between
two hearts is a road that leads straight back home. When you
pound this beat, it pounds you back. They could risk their lives in
the scam of the century or they could get real jobs—tough choice.
Ivy thought her best friend had the perfect house, the perfect family, the perfect life—so she took them. One love—two lives—she
could sell her body but not her heart. Into her perfect world comes
a perfect stranger—and suddenly ... nothing is perfect anymore.
She knew his face—his touch—his voice—she knew everything
about him ... but the truth. He looked like the ideal husband—he
seemed like the perfect father—that's just what they needed—but

that's not what they got. An older woman—a younger man—the possibilities were tantalizing: the reality was deadly. They had a passion so strong murder was the only way out. He wants to be tied down—she wants to be tied up—it's not what you think. Charming, seductive, deadly—your deepest secret is his most dangerous weapon. The only difference between a hunter and a killer is his eye. How do you lock the terror out when you've already locked the terror in? He's seen the future—now he has to kill it. One murder can change the world—one man can stop it. In a world on the brink of war, you either march to one tune or dance to another.

The Nimbus of His Fame etc.
Dreams about Kurt Cobain

Kurt and I were in a Karaoke bar. We were sitting in movie theater chairs, and the Karaoke stage was kinda far away from us. It was a really surreal thing. People were just walking around. It had a really spacey feel to it. He was not sitting next to me but next to next to me. Somebody was lip-synching to "Smells Like Teen Spirit," and I was, like, hey, man, do you know that they are the same exact chords from Blue Oyster Cult's "Godzilla"? Kurt and I got into this argument about it, and then he was like, man, how do you know that? I said, "I'm a musician," and he said okay. But then he just started going off: "Everybody's comin' down on me because I'm famous now." I was, like, well, I'm sorry. And then I said, "Well, I guess it's 'cause I'm jealous because you're not really that great a musician and you're famous and I really am a great musician and I'm just still struggling." And he said, "Okay, I can agree to that. I forgive you." It was kind of an exchange-of-angst thing. I angsted-out on him, because I didn't think he deserved it, and he angsted-out on me, saying why do you people have to angst-out on me?

—RAYMOND, 27

I dunno what the setting was, but I was kneeling, looking down the barrel of a gun, about to shoot myself in tribute to Kurt.

—RYAN, 17

Kurt was sort of a Jim Jones figure. It wasn't a jungle setting or anything, though, just an ordinary living room. Everyone was getting in line to commit suicide. The weird part is that when you got up to the head of the line to off yourself it wasn't Kool-Aid Kurt was handing out. It was Kaopectate.

—CHRIS, 31

I was at a Butthole Surfers show and it was like this big huge race-track, and that's where they were playing. I got up, 'cause I couldn't hear them; they weren't loud enough. We kept trying to get closer and closer. We finally found our way backstage and Kurt was back there. We had thought he died. He was sitting in this bathtub thing. We just hung out with him and we also hung out with the Nirvana bass player dude. They couldn't hear the Buttholes, either. It's kind of weird: every time I dream about the Buttholes I can't hear them.

—DAVE, 22

I was over at somebody's house at a party. There was a band play-ing a song by Hole, at which point I was reminded about Kurt's death and I started to cry and get upset about the whole thing. The weirdest thing is that I have never heard a song by Hole, but I knew that the band was doing a cover of Hole, anyway. I also remember thinking about doing covers of Nirvana songs—I'm in a band, and we've done covers of "Sliver," "Breed," and "Rape Me"—and thinking we are going to have to practice more to get them perfect.

—JULIAN, 19

I was at his house with a bunch of friends and it was kind of in-formal. It was kind of a dream house—a feeling of anarchy and domestic tranquility. I was made to feel very welcome. He was just playing music and singing, and I just remember waking up and thinking, wow, that's a beautiful new song, and looking at other friends of mine and thinking, this guy's great, this guy's the real thing. It was just kind of a stark and beautiful caterwauling, à la Kurt.

—DARREN, 26

I was in Kurt's house: a big, airy room, with wood floors and big windows. It had the sense of being high up, like we were looking

out over the lake maybe. Kurt was in the room along with Courtney Love and Eddie Vedder. It was a really big room, and it was like
each of us were in a corner. Courtney was really kind of agitated.
She was nervous and upset and excited and she kept talking about
a song that was supposed to be recorded really soon. I got the sense
that it was a Nirvana song. She was trying to talk to Kurt. He
was pretty aloof; I don't think he said anything. He was kind of at
the end of the room. He just didn't say much. Eddie was on the
other side of the room, kind of listening to Courtney, not really
saying much either, brooding, responding a little bit to Courtney.
But neither of them were really into what she was saying, and she
was very agitated. And there was a kind of sadness in the room, also
an urgency. Courtney was really trying to get things going, and
neither of them were helping her. I felt kind of bad for Courtney.
I wanted to help her. These two guys were being so unresponsive.
She was just so frantic, trying to get this new song recorded. She
really wanted to get this song recorded soon, otherwise it would
be too late. There was a real urgent sense, and Kurt didn't care.
She was dressed up, bright red lipstick, a white top—the way she
looked in those pictures of her in Rome. Eddie walked in circles,
rubbed his face, looked angst-ridden and brooding, like he does in
concert. Kurt was doing not much at all, kinda standing there; he
was there, but he wasn't really there.

—KIM, 34

You know those dreams where the hall lasts forever, and you finally
get to the door and you're really scared to open it? This was like that.
I was walking around Kurt's house and I started freaking out. I was
like, wait a minute, this is his house, what am I doing here? I went
to his room and I opened the door and he turned over and he
looked at me and said, "Life's a ball," and then pow—right in the
head. I was standing there and I saw him blow his head off. One
minute the house was all psychedelic colors; the next, it was black.

—MELINDA, 15

I was in the room when he was writing his suicide note. He was
trying really hard to think of what to say; he couldn't really write

very clearly, 'cause, you know, he was in a room with a gun. I was sorta watching from the outside of the room, looking in on him. I was just sort of observing the whole thing; I kind of came in through the window. Then he got the gun out and he put it next to the paper and just started writing with a normal pencil. Then he looked up at me and he was asking what he should say, and if this was really worth it. I was trying to give him advice, but I couldn't really think of anything to say except—well, what about your family, how are they going to deal with this, and he was like, yes, but I don't want my daughter to turn out like me. And I said I don't think having a father who committed suicide is going to do her much good, and he said yeah, finished his note, and looked up and said, "I'm sorry," like, to the world, sort of, and then blew himself away. He seemed really helpless. In the second before he shot himself, I saw this little boy inside, sort of crying for help, sort of a tragic hero thing.

—ARIEL, 15

I learned that Kurt had a terminal illness, and that Nirvana was playing a farewell show before he died. I went to the show (which seemed to be in a high school gym; it wasn't really clear) and sat next to Courtney. We watched the show, and afterwards we both sat and cried for a long time. While we were talking and crying— I remember her talking about Frances Bean, although I don't recall the context—it was announced over a loudspeaker that Kurt died. I don't remember anything after that.

—GRETA, 20

I was at my old high school back in Port Townsend and I was walking through the track field late at night, and my old boyfriend told me not to walk alone, but I did it, anyway, and I saw these three guys coming toward me and I'm like, "Have you guys seen Nirvana? I'm looking for Nirvana. Hasn't anybody seen Nirvana?" Like I had lost them. They're looking at me all weird. And then they started to attack me.

—MORGAN, 23

The etymology of the word *Nirvana* is given in various ways. According to Colebrooke (*Transactions of the Royal Asiatic Society*, Vol. I, p. 566), it comes from *va*, "to blow" like the wind, with the prefixed negative *nir*; hence it signifies a lull or calm, but as adjective "extinguished." Obry, *Du Nirvana indien*, p. 3, says: *Nirvanam en sanscrit signifie à la lettre extinction, telle que celle d'un feu.* ("Nirvanam in Sanskrit literally means extinction, e.g., as of a fire." Tr.) According to the *Asiatic Journal*, Vol. XXIV, p. 735, it is really *Neravana*, from *nera*, "without," and *vana*, "life," and the meaning would be *annihilatio*. In Spence Hardy's *Eastern Monachism*, p. 295, *Nirvana* is derived from *vana*, "sinful desires," with the negative *nir*. I. J. Schmidt, in his translation of the *History of the Eastern Mongolians*, p. 307, says that the Sanskrit *Nirvana* is translated into Mongolian by a phrase meaning "departed from misery," "escaped from misery." According to the same scholar's lectures at the St. Petersburg Academy, *Nirvana* is the opposite of *Samsara*, which is the world of constant rebirths, of craving and desire, of the illusion of the senses, of changing and transient forms, of being born, growing old, becoming sick, and dying. In Burmese the word *Nirvana*, on the analogy of other Sanskrit words, is transformed into *Nieban*, and is translated by "complete vanishing."

—ARTHUR SCHOPENHAUER[95]

I was pinning Kurt down on the bed and I thought I heard him laughing.

—MICHELLE, 20

The One We Truly Want

Crowds—who doesn't want to be part of a crowd?

"Dear Televiewer," the letter from Audience Selection Staff of Evansville, Indiana, begins. "We have taken the liberty of selecting you for an important role in television and are, herewith, inviting you to participate as a member of a hand-picked, special audience at our two-hour session 'Television Preview.' Two prerecorded typical half hours of television material (including programs and commercials) will be tested before several live groups across the country. Some of the material is being considered for national broadcast, and the producers, directors, sponsors and other people behind TV want to know your reactions. And later, if the shows are telecast, you will be able to feel that you were a member of the team that helped judge and evaluate them for their final release over television networks and stations."[96]

Like Madonna, "I want to be a big star. I want to be famous. I want everybody to love me."[97] And now here I am being offered "an important role in television." I don't even think of turning it down. I drive out to the Sea-Tac Marriott on a rainy Tuesday night.

In line ahead of me at the Marriott, one big guy asks another big guy if he wants to split a Butterfinger bar; the second big guy says, "Hell, we're not children. Let's each get our own." A disconcertingly large number of men here have sideburns, thin moustaches, and cowboy boots; several women wear low-cut party dresses. I feel like I've time-traveled back into a James M. Cain novel. The question I can feel all of us wanting to ask each other is: how have we been selected—do they somehow know we watch too much TV?

We're greeted at the door by a young woman who looks a lot like a chubbier Phoebe Cates, with bangs; have our tickets taken by a kid who looks like John Cusack wearing a sportcoat; and shown to our seats by a red-haired woman who looks like Annette O'Toole's younger sister. I keep asking myself: are my only points of reference the movies, or do these three people really look as much like their cinematic equivalents as I think they do? Pointing out a pretty-hard-to-miss cable on the floor, Annette O'Toole's Younger Sister explains to me, as if she were addressing Rain Man, "I didn't want you to trip."

While we're still settling into our seats, we hear an amplified voice chattering away: "That's sound information.... Hello, yes, well ... Am I on? ..." We couldn't see the speaker and at first everybody thought she was speaking to us, this flight-attendant-cum-businesswoman. Annette O'Toole's Younger Sister explains to us that this isn't part of the television preview but some other function from next door which is mistakenly being fed into "our" sound system; what's interesting is the brief moment of nervous laughter when we all acknowledge we'd first thought she was speaking to us—this invisible speaker—and we'd been pretty much willing to go along with the Orwellian experience.

Before watching the previews, we have lengthy surveys to answer. Each page of the first questionnaire implores us, "Please circle the *One* you truly want," then presents us with, for instance, thirty-one different kinds of margarine: Parkay, Parkay Soft, Parkay Squeeze Spread, Fleischmann's, Fleischmann's Light, Fleischmann's Unsalted, Shedd's Spread Country Crock, Shedd's Spread Country Crock Classic Quarters, Blue Bonnet, Blue Bonnet Light, Promise Extra Light, Imperial, Imperial Soft, Imperial Light, Imperial Diet, Imperial À La Mode, Gold-N-Soft, Gold-N-Soft Light, I Can't Believe It's Not Butter! Sweet Cream ... Which was the *One* I truly wanted? There is mystery and freedom here—I can, after all, write in my "favorite store brand"—but there's genius as well: "The booklet with your product selections is your entry for the prize drawings. If you do not make *one* selection from each category, we will not know what to include in your prize package." Somebody from the audience named Darren volunteers to choose three winning booklets from a basket as the three winners, and Phoebe Cates with Bangs instructs us to applaud him for performing this feat.

The first sitcom, *Love, Long Distance*, is about the marriage between a man who is a lumber company manager living in Philadelphia and a woman who is an archaeologist working at the Museum of Natural History in New York. The second sitcom, *Sisters*, is about the relationship between two sisters who live together—one a humorless and plain lawyer, the other lazy and luscious. In *Love, Long Distance*, we know the man is smart, even though he works for a lumber company, because he wears a *Williams College T-shirt*. In *Sisters*, we know the lazy sister's son is smart because he's starting *Yale Law School*. The famous East Coast thus functions as reassurance to the viewer that although these shows are shot in Los Angeles, they're not without a sort of New England weightiness.

The other fascinating thing about each of these shows is its plot. In *Love, Long Distance*, the archaeologist has a secret admirer sending her flowers and candy and making obscene calls, but the archaeologist thinks the lumberyard manager is just being extra nice to her. In *Sisters*, the lazy, luscious one nearly gets the humorless, plain one's maid deported, but it turns out the maid was born and raised in Brooklyn; she's only pretending to be an illegal alien. What's so extremely interesting about these stories is the way they completely back up on themselves, cancel themselves out, don't matter at all; they're like very difficult Zen koans, the answer to which can only emerge from a newly evolved understanding of the fundamental inconsequentiality of human existence.

In order not to disturb our concentration or objectivity, like conscientious teachers handling course evaluations, Phoebe Cates with Bangs, John Cusack Wearing a Sportcoat, and Annette O'Toole's Younger Sister have left the room during the showing of each sitcom. Now that the shows are over, the host and hostesses return and guide us through the questionnaires concerning *Sisters* and *Love, Long Distance*. John Cusack Wearing a Sportcoat notices that I've filled out my questionnaire with impossible alacrity and says, "Ooh, that was quick!"

There's one kiss-up in every class: one guy has to show the teachers and us how much he knows by saying, "Are you asking us whether we like the character or the actor *playing* the character?"

The dancer, the dance—who can tell the difference? This is the same guy who, later, when we're being quizzed on yet more products, insists on further clarification as to whether we're being asked specifically for our favorite liquid household *pine* cleaner or any kind? Caution to the wind, man, I think: any kind.

As the interminable night wears on, wears us down, tiny, tame mutinies occur. We're asked what our "favorite menstrual or premenstrual discomfort remedy" is, and the woman next to me stage-whispers, not very quietly, "Oh, lord, Jack Daniel's." "Do you own a dog or cat?" we're asked, and seemingly half the audience answers aloud, "Or does a dog or cat own you?" We watch a commercial for Folger's instant coffee and are then asked a dozen questions about how the coffee tastes, *based on what we've just seen.* "As opposed to reality," says my whole row.

Phoebe Cates with Bangs asks us a series of questions about AIDS, the homeless, capital punishment, and health care reform; she apologizes, "I know this is hard to think about after all of the commercials." And then, like ballplayers facing microphones thirty seconds after touching home plate, we're asked whether we find public opinion surveys such as the one we've just answered "worthwhile." You—who just did what you just did—what did you just do?

As if attempting to resist being an object by becoming a subject, I've been taking notes somewhat ostentatiously with my illuminated pen throughout the entire evening, and at the end of the program a gruff, heavyset, white-haired, older man—an M. Emmet Walsh look-alike—comes up to me and says, "I don't mean to be nosy or nothing, but why were you taking notes? Were you evaluating the programs or were you evaluating us?"

Just for the hell of it, I don't know why, I say, "I was evaluating you."

And here's the thing: not uncheerfully, he says, "Well, I hope we passed."

The Cultural Contradictions
of Late Capitalism

Crowds—who doesn't want to be part of a crowd? Driving west on
I-90, fifty miles from Rapid City, South Dakota, I pass sign after
sign advertising:

WALL DRUG CAFE SEATS 520

HOMEMADE PIE AND DONUTS WALL DRUG

FREE CAMPGROUND GUIDE WALL DRUG

BE A WALLFLOWER WALL DRUG

WALL MAKE YOU HAPPY WALL DRUG

WALL DRUG LIKE A MUSEUM

ROAST BEEF DINNERS WALL DRUG

BEST BET WALL DRUG

SHOPPING MALL WALL DRUG

SPIRIT OF '76 WALL DRUG

WALL DRUG AS TOLD BY WALL STREET JOURNAL

"Wall Drug signs grow thicker on the rolling prairie out here than
almost anything else," the *Wall Street Journal* article says. "Along
one 45-mile stretch of interstate highway, there are 53 of them."[98]

JEWELRY WALL DRUG

WALLCOME WALL DRUG

LOVE HER SHOW HER WALL DRUG

SILVER DOLLAR BAR WALL DRUG

WESTERN ART WALL DRUG

SINCE 1931 WALL DRUG

WALL DRUG OR BUST

STEAKS AND CAKES WALL DRUG

WALL DRUG AS SEEN ON TV SHOW WINNERS

COWBOY BOOTS WALL DRUG

RATTLESNAKE TIES WALL DRUG

WALL DRUG DINOSAUR EXIT

CAMPING SUPPLIES WALL DRUG

NEXT STOP WALL DRUG

BADLANDS HISTORY WALL DRUG

JUST AHEAD WALL DRUG

WALL DRUG AS TOLD BY FRONTIER MAGAZINE

EXIT 110 HERE COME THE WALL DRUG EXITS

WALL DRUG EXIT ¾ MILE

WALL DRUG NEXT EXIT ¼ MILE

In *Free Ice Water! The Story of Ted and Bill Hustead's Wall Drug*, Dana Close Jennings writes, "If you're normal—and a million people a year turn out to be normal as gooseberry pie—you'll decide as did the fella from Canada who told me, 'I decided anything advertising as much as this I had to see.'"[99] I have no idea what gooseberry pie is, but I want to be normal, so I stop in Wall, S.D., "the best-defended town in the world, being surrounded by fifty Minutemen missiles."[100] DON'T BE ALARMED WHEN A LOUD BELL RINGS, reads a little sign "just below the cactus seeds by the praying hands" in the block-long drugstore. IT JUST MEANS WE'VE CAUGHT ANOTHER SHOPLIFTER.[101]

Wall Drug

The Cultural Contradictions
of Early Capitalism
Postcards from Camp

I sleep over the bed so I won't have to make it. It's gotta be made
perfect. For breakfast I had 6 boxes of Sugar Pops, the small ones.

P.S. If you got the catcher's mitt with the Blue Chip Stamps,
don't tell me.

I lost my sweater today. I'll just hope it'll turn up in the Lost &
Found. I won 2 tennis contests for volleying against the wall.

P.S. Sorry about the sweater.

P.P.S. It will probably, hopefully be turned in.

Four great things happened on the Fourth of July: 1) in baseball I
got a triple, 2) in track I won the 100 yard dash (time: 13.6—not
very good), 3) in basketball I made 9 out of 10 set shots, 4) we had
a carnival.

There are two things I don't like up here: 1) flies, 2) food.

I made the top swimming group. The food is great. I don't sleep on
top of the bed anymore.

P.S. Please send gum in a package. It's allowed.

Please send me some chocolate chip cookies and gum. I was elected
captain of our team. The baseball coach said I had good form.

P.S. Sorry about the sloppy handwriting.

Thanks for the package. It was just great. I found my sweater. The
food is still great here. I had only 3 Sugar Pops boxes this morning.
The basketball coach elected me captain of our team.

If you have time before I come home, please send me the base-ball standings. The meals here aren't a third as good as your meals, Mom.[102]

Love Is Not a Consolation;
Love Is a Light

Food, they say, is a substitute for love; so, they should say, is every-thing else. When I bump into my ex-landlord outside the Com-munications Building, he tells me about a lecture a friend of his from Germany is giving later that day on campus. Karl is my ex-landlord not because I've moved but because he has: he moved out of the upstairs apartment shortly after I moved in downstairs. All summer, Karl had explained to me the nuances of the burglar alarm and meticulously packed boxes into his car; by the time his wife returned from an NEH seminar in anthropology at Princeton, he was gone. Now his ex-wife manages the property.

Karl teaches political science, and in the short time we lived in the same duplex, he struck me as ur-Professor: fuzzy beard, fuzzy hair, Birkenstocks, six pens tucked into the plastic pocket protec-tor attached to his white shirt. He listened to National Public Repetition day and night.

The title of the talk is "Images of Leaders in German, French, and American Television News," which sounds interesting enough until I walk into the room—a basement dungeon populated by twelve professors and graduate students eating bag lunches—and am handed a flyer, which contains an abstract of the talk:

Television news producers influence public evaluations of political leaders and issues partly by choosing how to display leaders' facial and bodily movements. Such "visual" quotations occupy almost identical amounts of time in Germany, France, and the U.S., about three minutes per newscast. Yet there are marked national differ-ences in the *form* of this daily dosage. U.S. channels present about 40% more political leaders per newscast, zoom individual leaders about 57% nearer to the viewer's eye, and reduce exposure time on screen by about 45% compared with French and German newscasts. The leaders' complex nonverbal activity was transcribed at high resolution into a time-series protocol. First analyses suggest some specific aspects of the nonverbal pattern that account for much of the variance in person perception. Lateral head flexion has a perplexingly strong influence on the attribution of personality traits, e.g., whether a leader is viewed as "arrogant, callous, stern, rejecting" or as "affectionate, thoughtful, acquiescent, caring."

I like that the word "form" is italicized for no particular reason, I like the Huxleyan metaphor of "daily dosage," and I love the confusion implicit in "perplexingly strong," but what does the rest of it mean—"time-series protocol"? "lateral head flexion"? I haven't a clue.

Karl introduces his friend and colleague, Siegfried Frey, as a psychologist, engineer, political scientist, and "student of the impact of pharmaceuticals on human behavior." He also teaches in the psychology department at the University of Duisburg. Karl says he's "looking forward with bated breath to finding out the significance of lateral head flexion." So are we all.

Siegfried Frey has a perplexingly strong resemblance to Mikhail Gorbachev, only younger and without the birthmark. He begins his presentation by flashing onto an overhead projector three quotations that seem uncontroversial to the point of being self-evident:

There is no meaning in a message except what people put into it. When we study communication, therefore, we study people.

—WILBUR SCHRAMM

In everyday life, we respond to gestures with an extreme alertness, and one might almost say, in accordance with an elaborate and secret code that is written nowhere, known by none, and understood by all.

—EDWARD SAPIR

We look at a person and immediately a certain impression of his

character forms itself in us. A glance, a few spoken words are sufficient to tell us a story about a highly complex matter.

—SOLOMON ASCH

Dr. Frey explains that a linguist in Paris, a government professor
in New Hampshire, and he had each monitored two television stations in France, the United States, and Germany for a full month—
March 1987. They have gathered more than four thousand individual clips; they have a data base of eleven and a half hours. There
are amusing little statistical revelations: French television news has
the longest delay until the first leader is presented, as well as the
longest intervals between sequences of political leaders; U.S. news
programs rarely display any film clips longer than twenty seconds,
while Germany and France often have lengthier samples; U.S.
news rarely displays more than one political leader simultaneously,
which contradicts, to my mind, anyway, Dr. Frey's flattering asser-
tion that "the more democratic approach of the U.S." is responsi-
ble for the fact that nearly twice as many political leaders appear
on U.S. television news than on French or German programs;
there is no systematic difference in the nonverbal communication
of Qaddafi and Reagan.

But the two-headed lady that has enticed us into the circus tent,
what we are looking forward to with bated breath is, of course, lateral head flexion. What in the world is it and how does it ramify?
It's really interesting and it ramifies across the board. On the overhead projector Dr. Frey shows us a transparency he has made of the
October 20, 1986 cover of *Time*. The large cover lines are:

NO DEAL

STAR WARS SINKS THE SUMMIT

Reagan's head is tilted slightly to the right in his characteristic
Mr. Smith Goes to Washington posture, that is, displays lateral head
flexion. Gorbachev's head is straight up, chin out.

A few weeks later, *Time* had printed a letter from a reader who
thought that the pictures on the cover "said it all": Gorbachev was
"arrogant, hard, uncompromising," while Reagan "showed concern,

frustration, and disappointment." Dr. Frey's research indicates that for men and for women, for blacks and whites, for children and adults, for Japanese and Westerners, "lateral head flexion" has a "noticeable impact" upon a viewer's evaluation of the person being depicted. Not just Gorbachev but anyone whose head is straight up is identified with such adjectives as "proud, aloof, self-confident, arrogant, self-assured, callous, stern, stiff, conceited"; not just Reagan but anyone whose head is tilted ever so slightly toward the viewer is perceived as being "humble, kind, sad, thoughtful, alert, friendly, sympathetic, tense, tender, vulnerable." According to Dr. Frey, artists for centuries have used lateral head flexion in a "manneristic way" to control the viewer's response to figures. He flashes photographs and drawings at us, and it's simply uncanny the degree to which the slight tilt of a person's head determines one's reading of that person's character.

Dr. Frey refuses to speculate on the "possible psychological semantics of lateral head flexion." It's simply a "curious coincidence of nonverbal communication." I, on the other hand, have always been a big fan of the wildly sweeping generalization, and I ask my fellow colloquium-attendees whether one couldn't at least speculate that this difference in how viewers respond is related in some sense to yielding a stance of authority, i.e., to an adult acting childlike; Reagan always seemed to be trying to look so boyish whenever he dropped his head in that way. Dr. Frey says this is interesting but unverifiable. A woman to my immediate left catches the spirit and suggests that a viewer looks favorably on someone whose head is tilted because such a posture suggests a mother nursing an infant. Unverifiable, says Dr. Frey, but interesting.

Then Karl, who until now seems to have been busy eating the lunch he has brought to the colloquium, brings his right hand—slowly, and with great care and patience—from a vertical position into a horizontal position until it's lying snugly on top of his left hand, and proceeds to offer two tentative theses concerning the symbolic power of lateral head flexion: first, that tilting your head suggests that you're trying to see things from another perspective; and, second, that it's a physically intimate gesture—implying, as it does, a movement from the vertically isolated to the horizontally intertwined. It's by far the most astonishing thing I've heard in an already fairly eye-opening afternoon. It seems not only interesting and verifiable but the language itself by which to describe what he misses about marriage.

Tom Collicott

Tom Collicott

Desire

The peso is very low. I wake up at night to lizards dancing on the ceiling fan. I go down to the lobby for lunch, and a cow is tied to the balustrade. I walk into town, and for a hundred yards every child I see is crippled, hopping along the sidewalk with wooden arms and legs. Dead dogs, scrawny cats, babies on bamboo in the dirt, endlessly circling taxis—even the birds seem drunk. The Pacific Ocean is so close that when the shades are open, the picture window in the hotel bedroom frames boats like a TV screen. I look out the picture window, and oil tankers coming into port look like toy boats. Then the toy boats start leaking oil and suddenly they seem a lot more like real boats. The oil is so thick I can't swim in the ocean: I swim in the pool until I get an ear infection, which is treated by a doctor who—deep in preparation for his first trip to Spain next month—wants to hear only about my experience with prostitutes in Barcelona (e.g., at the end of a long block of raven-haired women sitting on windowsills hung a shingle for the *urólogo*).

Why We Live at the Movies

That is why we, snatched from sudden freedom, are able to
communicate only through this celluloid vehicle that has
immortalized and given a definite shape to our formless gestures;
we can live as though we had caught up with time and avoid the
sickness of the present, a shapeless blur as meaningless as a
carelessly exposed roll of film. There is hardness and density
now, and our story takes on the clear, compact shape of the plot
of a novel.

—JOHN ASHBERY

Whenever my then-girlfriend and I would go to plays, they would
inevitably strike us as odd and antediluvian in their absence of a
mechanical framing device. We would spend entire afternoons and
evenings in cineplexes, sneaking from movie to movie, lugging vats
of popcorn and soda. We'd always stay until the absolute end of the
credits—the studio logo. The appeal for her was the "sensory over-
load" of image, music, and speech. What I love the most is that it's
almost the only time I cry. The worse the movie, the more I cry.

Someone somewhere says that a darkened movie theater reminds
us of being in the womb and that the images we see evoke the

worlds we dreamed before we were born.[103] This seems to me to be simply true: by far my favorite moment in a movie theater comes when the final trailer is over, the last house lights dim off, and the otherwise dormant right side of my brain takes over completely.

During the trailers, my girlfriend and I would compete to see who could whisper first into the other person's ear the name of the movie being previewed. I would almost always win, because I read movie reviews the way other people eat candy; I read movie reviews the way I eat candy. We were members of video stores all over Seattle, and video clubs all across the country. On long weekends we'd choose a film that bore rewatching and watch it on an endless loop, until it felt physically painful to walk around outside the environment of the movie.

She was a genius at following and predicting plot developments; I was a great one for tracing themes and analyzing motive: she'd explain to me what happened, and I'd explain to her what it all meant. Together, we felt like Fellini. At first our worst arguments would occur when I'd start analyzing the movie the moment we walked out of the theater. Then our worst arguments would occur when one of us was preternaturally attracted to one of the stars of the movie. Daniel Day-Lewis, for instance. Annabella Sciorra, for instance. Daniel Day-Lewis, for instance.

Whenever we had people over for dinner, invariably we talked about movies all during dinner, then watched movies afterward. If people came over and somehow we managed not to watch a movie and our guests left before ten, sometimes she or I would race out to the video store and return with our fix. What was this jolt we came to crave so deeply? I'd read a book, then she'd read it, and we'd talk about it. Or, out on a drive, one of us would read a story aloud to the other. Or we'd read different books together in bed. It was nice, but it wasn't the same.

The glory of watching a movie with someone else is the illusion that the same experience is being simultaneously imprinted upon both participants' brains. It's very romantic, like simultaneous orgasm or double suicide. You (who are so different from me and who just saw what I just saw) thought and felt what I thought and felt, didn't you? The crime you saw (your understanding of the crime you saw) didn't differ from the crime I saw (my understanding of the crime I saw), did it? She would always check to see if I had been crying.

The crucial moment in Hemingway's *The Garden of Eden* occurs when David and Catherine come to understand that everything they've been doing has been an attempt to keep alive, or perhaps to resurrect, the feelings they felt when they first fell in love with each other. Movies are the synthetic injection of these feelings: the whole world comes into focus and seems alluring and dangerous; our lives, which aren't lived on the grand scale, are lived on the grand scale. Give me the heated-up myth, each of us practically prays to the screen: make life seem coherent and big and free of my qualifying consciousness.

The Confessions

Rousseau might as well be talking about sex in solitude when he describes the process by which he writes. When he's "alone and at work," his ideas ferment until they excite and heat him. His heart beats fast. "In the midst of this excitement," he's unable to see, unable to write, and obliged to wait until the confusion clears up and "everything takes its proper place." Classical dramatic structure is an accurate, if rather dry, diagram of the sexual experience. Writing is directly analogous to sex, and given his preoccupations, especially to masturbation for Rousseau. He can't write until the tension of arousal has been released. Confessional writing and masturbation fantasy are Rousseau's internalized expressions of revenge upon society for its use of language and sex for merely legitimate purposes: namely, communication and procreation. Jean-Jacques wants to be the only person who has access to the pleasures of language and sex. "If I had known how to wait first and then to restore in all their beauty the things represented in my brain, few writers would have surpassed me," Rousseau writes, but surely he realizes the impossibility of reversing the creative and sexual patterns so that he arrives at beauty before subjecting himself to chaos.[104]

The One We Truly Want
A Brief Survey of Ideal Desire

The greatest poverty is not to live
In a physical world, to feel that one's desire
Is too difficult to tell from despair.
—WALLACE STEVENS

Pornography isn't, in my experience and opinion, a substitute for closeness; it's a revel in distance.

Our fifth-grade social studies teacher had supposedly once appeared in *Playboy*. This rumor could never be confirmed or denied, but for the first time in my life I got a C: no one in that class—boys or girls—could concentrate on anything except Miss Acker. "Petite Nancy Spiess," "a bunny of Detroit," "a motorcycle buff," was the first figure in a magazine to whom I ever masturbated.[105] Those silver fingernails, that green bikini bottom—I couldn't stop imagining her in the buff, on the back of a motorcycle.

My parents hired a guy named Gil to paint the inside of the house; after Gil left, my mother discovered the word "Fuck" etched into the new white paint in the dining room. I'd never seen my father so infuriated. Had my parents underpaid or somehow mistreated Gil, and had this been his underhanded revenge? He adamantly denied it, offering to return to rectify the problem. Had my sister or I done it? We insisted we hadn't, and I'm confident we were telling the truth. Although over time the inscription lost its hold on my father's imagination, "Fuck" remained—if faintly—and continued to cast a subtle, mysterious spell over the dining room for the remainder of my childhood.

In high school, I couldn't keep looking at a girl once she'd seen me looking at her, i.e., looked back. This wasn't a lot of help to me on the dating scene. Saturday nights, during my adolescence, were exhausting: first Sally Struthers, then Mary Tyler Moore, then Suzanne Pleshette—all on CBS. By ten P.M., my bruised and abused and battered penis was relieved *Mannix* was on.

In a college literature class, the professor asked us what scenes represented genuine desire—the scenes of the main character going to pornographic movies or the scenes of the main character making love with his wife? "The scenes of the main character going to pornographic movies," I said.

I'm particularly partial to the ink screens covering certain words and certain body parts in ads for films and phone sex in porn magazines. It's the most transparent ruse, but I find it always works. Once, flipping through the pictures in a dirty magazine, I noticed, on one woman's leg and back, a couple of blotches marked with grease-pencil circles, which, rather than being responded to by the photo retoucher, had, through negligence, remained, like a critique of false premises.

I went through a Seka phrase—did any straight American man not, in the early eighties, go through a Seka phase?—until I noticed that, in group shots with other women, Seka was granted the rare privilege of not having to make eye contact with the viewer; even for me, this seemed too remote a spot from which to worship the goddess. The fantasy was that she disdained you until you fucked her into loving you.

In my local convenience store, cigarette ads with open-mouthed women are hung just inside the door at, I never fail to notice, at crotch level.

When the man behind the counter at the blue-movie store asks if he can help me find anything, I say, "Just browsing."

He replies, "That's what I said four years ago, and look at me now."

I "replay a porno film, paid for a quarter at a time, bad milk spilled in a booth."[106]

The porn star Nina Hartley says, "They're masturbating and they can't mask their eyes. You can see their trepidations. They come to me with their expectations and their desires, and they're very fearful. Their eyes are filled with a mixture of erotic energy, openness, hope, and fear. Vulnerability. But some of them are completely comfortable with the whole thing. They're the funnest."[107]

I keep asking a woman in a peep show to do this, mouth that, look a certain way, until she finally says, "What do you want, a girlfriend or a show?"

Immediately after the breakup of a relationship, I became a fan for a while of a massage parlor called Misfits. I never went there, but I enjoyed looking at their ad in the phone book; calling and hanging up; thinking about the perfect pun of their name: Miss/Fits—a little relief in a tight spot for the alienated man.

When I was a little kid, I read in the *San Francisco Chronicle* that the stripper Carol Doda was "statuesque." I didn't know what the word meant, but in one important feature my babysitter resembled Carol Doda, so I asked her whether she was statuesque. She said she didn't know what that meant, but we could look it up.

When I was a little kid, I was a very good baseball player, but I actually preferred to go over to the park across from our house, sit atop the hill, and watch Little Leaguers, kids my age or younger, play for hours. "What's the matter with you?" my father would ask me. "You should be out playing. You shouldn't be watching." I don't know what's the matter with me—why I'm adept only at distance, why I feel so remote from things, why life feels like a rumor—but my father was right: playing has somehow always struck me as a fantastically unfulfilling activity.

Radio

"Do you know what I hate about not having a radio?" my upstairs neighbor asks.

"What?" I say. She'd been back a day or two from Vancouver, where her antenna had been snapped off.

"You feel like you could be driving along, a nuclear disaster could occur, and you wouldn't even have contact."

"Contact?" I say. "Contact with what?"

"Everyone else."

Last Lines

It Isn't the Suspense That Is Killing Us

I know why you're here; let's go on with it.
 I don't have time to play games, so if you got something to tell
me . . .
 My secretary said it was urgent.
 So what's going on between you and her?
 I'm sure there's a point to all of this.
 Look, I'll make it easy for you.
 And here's the beauty part . . .
 I don't expect any sympathy from you—I never wanted to do
this to you—but I thought I had no choice.
 I don't want to hurt you, but I will if I have to.
 I got something I got to tell you.
 The moral is—there is no moral.
 Let me make it easy for you.
 You could have saved yourself a lifetime of grief.
 There's something I must tell you.
 I'm a dead man now.

Epilogue
How to Make a Paper Hat

Paper hats have been worn by printers, paper-makers, and type-founders for centuries, and are still worn by some. This is the way hats were made in the nineteenth century: Take a double edge of a newspaper. Turn it so the fold is at the top. Turn the folded edge to the center to make two triangles and a flap. Take the TOP SHEET ONLY of the flap, fold it in half, and fold it to the center. Fold up the outside corners of the bottom flap, then fold the flap itself up and tuck it into the brim above. Fold the top down and tuck that into the brim, too. Pick up the corners and pick up the cap by its brim, open it out, and flatten it. Fold in the two corners and tuck them under the brim. Open out the hat and square it.

Notes

1. George W. S. Trow, *Within the Context of No Context* (New York, 1981), 7.

2. Cf. J. F. Powers, quoted in Mervyn Rothstein, "Catholic Author Deeply Fascinated by the Priesthood," *New York Times*, 15 September 1988, C19: "There are all kinds of imperfections we have to live with, which original sin explains.... There are people who don't see it that way. They feel that if you buy a bad pair of shoes you simply shouldn't buy that brand again. But I see these things as the essence of mortality, little grace notes of mortality. And if you say, 'That's life,' well, you're right. That's life."

3. Quotations from Vladimir Nabokov, *Speak, Memory* (New York, 1966), 19; Nabokov, *The Real Life of Sebastian Knight* (London, 1945).

4. Pauline Kael calls Charles Martin Smith "likeably sane" in Kael, *5001 Nights at the Movies* (New York, 1991), 710.

5. Bob Balaban, quoted in Judy Klemesrud, "He's Making a Career of Projecting Intelligence," *New York Times*, 10 January 1982, D28: "I think I could play a romantic leading man. I'd like to have bigger parts, and I've been offered a couple of leading roles. But I haven't liked them. When you're the star of a movie that is not a very good movie, that can be disastrous for you."

6. This synopsis is adapted from Pauline Kael's review of the film in Kael, *5001 Nights*, 20.

7. Bob Balaban, *Close Encounters of the Third Kind Diary* (Paradise, Calif., 1978), 106–107.

8. Cf. Leo Braudy, *The Frenzy of Renown* (New York, 1986), 589.

9. Letter from Bart Kercher to the author, 7 September 1989.

10. Israel Shenker, "Perelman Shaken Up by Florida's Charms," *New York Times*, 27 April 1974, 25.

11. Richard Todd, "The Missing Middle," *New York Times Magazine*, 1 February 1976, 10, 11, 56, 60, 64, 65. Actually, interestingly (to me,

anyway), I ended up being wrong: when, nearly twenty years later, I asked the photographer, Ted Polumbaum, to confirm what I'm sure he thought was my paranoid theory, he showed me all his contact sheets from the shoot, and I couldn't find myself in any of them. Not only that, but Tad Kinney possessed neither tortoiseshell glasses nor an Exeter jaw. Still, the papers and notebooks at the very far bottom left of the frame?—they're mine; I'm certain of it.

12. Ira Berkow, "No Hefty Lunch for Beefy Gregg," *New York Times*, 30 June 1990, 43.

13. Letter from Judy Jordan to the author, 24 June 1991.

14. Phone message from Rick Telander to the author, 22 June 1992.

15. "I had a consultant say to me once, on viewing a piece, where the sound cut ran thirteen seconds, 'It's too long, that's much too long.' And I said, 'How did we arrive at six seconds?' He said, 'Because we taught them that six seconds is all they should have to listen to. We taught them that.'" Aaron Brown, former Seattle television anchorman, on *Murrow: Broadcast Journalism in the Puget Sound*, KCTS, Public Broadcasting System, Seattle affiliate, 28 August 1990.

16. Cf. Dick Schaap, "'Scary *Is* Good,'" *Parade*, 13 September 1992, 4.

17. Henry James, "The Middle Years," *The Short Stories of Henry James*, ed. Clifton Fadiman (New York, 1945), 315.

18. Cf. letter from Bruce Brooks to the author, n.d.: "How fucking stupid. First of all, I told you several months ago (and very carefully— because I wanted to forestall this very sort of awkwardness) that your experience with and evaluation of TM was your own business, and you should not feel any loyalty because of my own personal convictions about it. I told you I told you I told you; start for your own reasons, continue or quit for your own reasons, don't feel any connection between me and your practice. Having made that (I thought) clear, I felt free to offer my comments in response to your questions and to show my gladness that you were getting beneficial results. I never gave any sign that I had made your personal practice or opinion of TM a condition or even a connection to our friendship, and if you think back, you will see this, I'm sure. True, I think TM is hot stuff; true, I do not hide my enthusiasm, based on my own experience; true, I answered your questions and shared my enthusiasm with you. Every teacher of the TM program has learned that he must be careful with friends who are starting to meditate, to protect both that person's practice and the friendship against completely artificial connections. I was this careful with you and with other friends who had started; whether they have kept meditating or not has nothing to do with

whether or not they have remained friends. A TM teacher wants no one to stop meditating because that person comes to dislike him, and he wants no one to dislike him because they have come to stop meditating, so we are good and careful to keep the lines clear. You think back; I know damn well that I never invited the kind of association you have now proposed, because I was wary of it from the beginning and, professionally, was careful. When, in your letter last spring, you said you had stopped, my thought was, quite simply, oh, his loss. That's all. As for your very interesting ideas about TM's conditions and limitations versus what you wanted, I was in fact interested in discussing with you a lot of points that applied, but I was unsure whether or not the discussion might seem to you like dogmatic coercion, and had not decided to open it yet. You start, you stop; it's your business. You could sell your mantra to the highest bidder on *The Tonight Show*, and it would be your loss, not mine. If this sounds callous, it is so as an alternative to the kind of meddlesome advocacy of which I believe your letter would have accused me, had I read it.

"Your doubts about me are consistent with your tendency to look for exterior explanations that contradict your own inner certainties. You know very damn well how I feel about you, and in spite of your tendency to equivocate toward negating possibilities, you must feel in your heart and soul how secure and stable and remarkable the friendship between us is. So, by coming into all of this baroque speciousness about 'rejection,' you are not only going against evidence I have given you of my devotion but also the clear confirmation of that evidence from inside yourself. The ease with which one throws off intuition is a measure of such trustlessness, and the rococo elegance of these formulations shows that intelligence is not always the servant of the heart's certainty. In my case, for a long time, things I could think would always take ascendancy over contradictory things I could feel. I am not ascribing a similar problem to you exactly, but it's a possibility. Feeling can indeed be trusted to endure and serve as strength that is not shaken by little furies and matchstick machineries of doubt and pique. Maybe the friendships you have had before slip and vanish and nova in little frenzies of ecstasy, but not this one. I suspect that your other friendships are as strong as ours, in fact, and have not served as evidence of amity's frailness; perhaps you treat some of them to the same suspicion that you have chucked at ours, but the indignity is yours, not the friendships'. This durability is something everybody has to figure out for himself, but it is one of the great revelations and you had better open up to it. There is nothing like relaxing and knowing that your loves are soft and will not be threatened. To persist in a romantic or tragic thrall of dark uncertainty is an insult to yourself and your friends. Or, at least, it will damn sure be an insult to me next time you manifest it. A man has come to the point of trusting himself. A boy does not trust himself. It is that simple, truly. From not trusting oneself comes the insidious horror of, among other things, insecurity, which frankly is an affliction to which you are prey in spades. I think you had better apologize to the amazing human being that you are and decide to give yourself some trust. From which, very easily, you come to trust others. Like me."

19. Quentin Tarantino, quoted in Peter McAlevey, "All's Well That Ends Gruesomely," *New York Times Magazine*, 6 December 1992, 81.

20. Quotations from Jean-Jacques Rousseau's *Confessions*, trans. J. M. Cohen (New York, 1977), 118.

21. Joseph Schildkraut, *My Father and I* (New York, 1959), 108, 129, 153.

22. Ibid., 30.

23. David Shields, *Dead Languages* (New York, 1989), 86.

24. Schildkraut, *My Father*, 34, 81.

25. His other films include *Marie Antoinette, Idiot's Delight, Orphans of the Storm, Cleopatra, The Road to Yesterday, The Garden of Allah, Flame of the Barbary Coast, The Man in the Iron Mask, Northwest Outpost, Mr. Moto Takes a Vacation, Souls at Sea, The Crusades, The King of Kings,* and *The Shop Around the Corner.* He's invariably self-regarding, studied, stiff, grave, dignified, and yet also prone, regardless of role, to a truly astonishing amount of bowing-and-scraping.

26. Quoted in Kristine McKenna, "A Monster Called Sting: The *Rolling Stone* Interview," *Rolling Stone*, 1 September 1983, 15.

27. Paul Avery, "Big UC Campus Drug Case—Hunt for 'Mr. Big,'" *San Francisco Chronicle*, 12 June 1965, 1, 3.

28. Quoted in Dave Lafontaine, "Real Twin Peaks Town Hides Dark Secrets of Its Own," *Star*, 10 April 1990, 30.

29. Quoted in Jennifer Land, "Woody Harrelson Becomes a Cowboy," *Vancouver Sun*, 12 July 1994, C10.

30. Quoted in Lynn Hirschberg, "The Four Brushmen of the Apocalypse," *Esquire*, March 1987, 77.

31. Philip Roth, *Goodbye, Columbus* (Boston, 1959), 3.

32. Spalding Gray, *Swimming to Cambodia* (New York, 1985), 47–48.

33. Michael J. Fox, discussing co-star Christina Vidal and quoted in "Seen, Heard, Said," *Seattle Times*, 3 June 1993, E1.

34. Debi Mazar, quoted in Jill Gerston, "The Know-It-All New Yorker of *Civil Wars*," *New York Times*, 27 September 1992, sec. 2, p. 31.

35. Hendrik Hertzberg, "California with a New York Edge," *New York Times Book Review*, 17 May 1992, 39.

36. Alan King, quoted in Glenn Collins, "The Man Who Grew Up Talkative," *New York Times*, 19 May 1993, B5.

37. George Vecsey, "Sir Charles Is Gonna Be Outrageous," *New York Times*, 27 April 1993, B11.

38. Blaine Newnham, "Aggressive Sonics Run Across Suns' Weakness," *Seattle Times*, 31 May 1993, C6.

39. Benoit Benjamin, quoted in "Sideline Chatter," *Seattle Times*, 3 July 1993, B2.

40. Andrew Sullivan, "Washington Diarist: Go West," *New Republic*, 18 October 1993, 50.

41. "Not Caffeinated," *New Yorker*, 27 September 1993, 35.

42. Arlene Croce, "The Spelling of *Agon*," *New Yorker*, 12 July 1993, 84.

43. Bruce Weber, "Converging on Nowhere with Families and Fliers," *New York Times*, 6 July 1993, A8.

44. George Vecsey, "It's a Trend: Even Jordan Is Not Enough to Stop It," *New York Times*, 26 May 1993, B8.

45. "The President's Locks—Grid and Curly," editorial, *New York Times*, 22 May 1993, sec. 1, p. 18.

46. Claire Smith, "Now Starring in the Carnival's Sideshow, It's the New York Mets," *New York Times*, 22 April 1993, B17.

47. Joe Sexton, "Lost in a City He Calls Home," *New York Times*, 25 April 1993, sec. 8, p. 1.

48. Lorne Michaels, quoted in Elizabeth Kolbert, "New Job for NBC's Laugh Master: Fill the Late-Night Letterman Gap," *New York Times*, 23 February 1993, C16.

49. Smith, "Now Starring," B17.

50. Toni Morrison, quoted in John Leonard, "All That Jazz," *New York*, 21 and 28 December 1992, 72.

51. Lorne Michaels, quoted in Elizabeth Kolbert, "New Job for NBC's Laugh Master," C16.

52. Toni Morrison, paraphrased in John Leonard, "All That Jazz," 72.

53. John Guare, paraphrased in Mel Gussow, "Chasing Serendipity in New York City," *New York Times*, 20 May 1993, C1.

54. Rudolph Giuliani, quoted in Todd S. Purdum, "Rudolph Giuliani and the Color of Politics in New York," *New York Times Magazine*, 25 July 1993, 25.

55. Smith, "Now Starring," B17.

56. Sexton, "Lost in a City," sec. 8, p. 3.

166

57. George Vecsey, "Can Bonilla Get Along in New York?," *New York Times*, 16 April 1993, B9.

58. Malcolm Moran, "Bulls Make It 3 in a Row for a 3-2 Advantage," *New York Times*, 3 June 1993, B7.

59. Vecsey, "It's a Trend," B8.

60. Thom Jones, "Cold Snap," *New Yorker*, 21 June 1993, 83.

61. Cf. letter from Michael Cunningham to the author, 11 July 1988: "Should you move to New York? Are you missing anything important by *not* living in New York? I don't have an easy answer to that. Everyone I know seems to fall into one of two categories: those who live in New York and want to get out, and those who don't live in New York and worry that they should. That's semi-facetious. I'm the last one to take matters of geography lightly. I must say that though I may very well end up spending my dotage in this city, it's a hard place to live and, possibly more important, a hard place to work. I find I haven't been all that productive here during the last year, mainly because a) even the simplest life, involving tap water and a movie every other Saturday, is expensive, almost mysteriously so, ergo much energy goes into earning a living; and b) if you are prone, as I am, to venture beyond tap water and biweekly movies, it's very distracting. The latter is largely personal, because not everyone is as distractible as I am, but I got five times more work done during a year in a Greek village, population twelve. I know, of course, that the question about living in New York isn't entirely a practical one. I had no intention of spending the next forty years in any Greek village, population twelve. And, yes, New York has a sense of weight—a feeling of the history of the culture being made—that's a hell of a lot subtler in most other places. No doubt about it, there's something distinctly satisfying and, all right, *enlivening* about being surrounded by so many people who are doing something other than punching time at the cement factory. Not to mention what those people are wearing, and what they've done to their hair.

"It's an important place; by learning your way around it, you feel important yourself. And I suppose that sense of magnitude must be a help in writing, both in that it nourishes the simple egotism that's a crucial ingredient in fiction writing (you know what I mean—the conviction that one has the *right* to tell a story, and that it's worth people's time to listen), and that it keeps driving home the unmistakable fact that life is big enough to be worth writing about. Not that either of those states is unattainable in Sioux Falls. But in New York they fall like rain. You should know, though (you probably know already), that lately it's been getting ever more polarized: on one hand, there are the rich and protected; on the other, there are the poor and the furious. Sometimes it's hard to separate the continuing, customary complaints of New Yorkers from more urgent concerns, but more and more of my friends, including some real dyed-in-the-wool types whose idea of a faraway place is 95th Street, have been feeling uneasy here. It's been feeling dangerous in a general sense, as opposed to the individual fear of mugging or burglary. This particular fear stems from the sight of people in sable stepping around people who are starving, and from being asked by thirty different people (not exaggerating), some of whom are very pissed off, for money while you go about your errands. In short, it feels like it's going to blow.

"I used to get irritated here, but I don't remember ever feeling uneasy. Lately I do. And the expense factor has a direct effect, too, on unwealthy types like writers. As I said before—evidently this is a point I feel needs to be driven in with a sledgehammer—there just aren't cheap places to live anymore. Most of the artists I know live deep in Brooklyn or Queens or Hoboken, which by my lights share most of Manhattan's irksome qualities without many of its mitigating factors. At bottom the question is unanswerable. Who knows what kind of experience you'd have? Am *I* glad to be here? Not particularly. I really do believe it's at a dark spot in its history now, assuming that cities undergo depressions and other moods as people do. Will I leave? Who knows? If I decide to stay, I'll move to one of the little towns in the Hudson River Valley and commute. Like the suburbanite I've always been at heart."

62. The incidents involving, and the quoted statements by and about, John Melendez that are not taken from Degen Pener, "Egos & Ids," *New York Times*, 5 July 1992, sec. 9, p. 4, or John Martel, "M.C. Stammer," *Rolling Stone,* 5 September 1991, 95–96, are taken from various television episodes of *The Howard Stern Show*. References to Joey Adams, Liz Smith, Walter Mondale, Morton Downey Jr.: Martel, "M.C. Stammer," 95.

63. Martel, "M.C. Stammer," 95–96.

64. Pener, "Egos & Ids," 4.

65. "King of the Interns," "world's oldest intern," "stuttering baboon," "There is no show on television.... What a mess!": Martel, "M.C. Stammer," 96.

66. Tourette's: ibid.

67. Susan Sontag, foreword to Michel Leiris's *Manhood: A Journey from Childhood into the Fierce Order of Virility* (Chicago, 1992), ix.

68. Martel, "M.C. Stammer," 96.

69. Pener, "Egos & Ids,"4.

70. Martel, "M.C. Stammer," 95–96.

71. Pener, "Egos & Ids," 4.

72. Melendez was apparently the beneficiary of substantial speech therapy before serving as one of the panelists on the recent, short-lived, late-night gabfest *Last Call.* Without (most of) his stutter, he quickly became wearisome and unlikable.

73. Pener, "Egos & Ids," 4.

74. Martel, "M.C. Stammer," 95.

75. Vincent Terrace, ed., *The Complete Encyclopedia of Television* (New York, 1986), 387.

76. "Off the Deep End," *Time,* 9 June 1958, 61.

77. Venkat Ramani, M.D., "Audiogenic Epilepsy Induced by a Specific Television Performer," *New England Journal of Medicine* 325, no. 2 (11 July 1991), 134–135.

78. "Overheard," *Newsweek,* 10 September 1990, 13.

79. Cf. "Language Is a Virus," author's letter to the editor, *Village Voice,* 6 February 1990, 4. "In 'Strange Angels,' Laurie Anderson's contribution to 'The Wannabe Decade: A Special Issue,' she writes: 'And it was like the two tears of kitsch: the first tear says: Look at all you wonderful Americans. And the second tear says: And look how sensitive we all are for noticing.' This idea and image are taken directly from Milan Kundera's discussion of kitsch in *The Unbearable Lightness of Being,* in which he writes, 'Kitsch causes two tears to flow in quick succession. The first tear says: How nice to see children running on the grass! The second tear says: How nice to be moved, together with all mankind, by children running on the grass! It is the second tear that makes kitsch kitsch.' Shouldn't Ms. Anderson's debt here have been acknowledged?" Laurie Anderson's reply: "I'm not sure I'm glad that Kundera seems to be lurking in the back of my mind near where I've filed art history. The two tears of kitsch was an idea I thought I'd picked up from a long ago discussion of German art. Obviously not. Thank you for pointing this out."

80. Correspondence between the author and John Updike, 23 April 1991: "Do you recognize the phrase 'gliding along on the light ice of their gifts' as something you've written? I thought it was from 'Tomorrow and Tomorrow and So Forth,' but I didn't find it there and I haven't had any luck looking through your other work, either. If you do recognize the passage, I would certainly appreciate a nudge in the right direction." Updike: "There is some ice-skating in the middle of an old essay about my boyhood, 'The Dogwood Tree,' and then toward the end of that same piece, but the phrasing isn't close to what you have. And 'Thin Ice' is the title of one of the chapters in *Couples.* What you quote might come from

a review, with 'thin' instead of 'light' and 'talents' instead of 'gifts,' but it doesn't ring much of a bell. Sorry. Still, even negative input has its scientific worth."

81. "Karen's Kids," *60 Minutes*, CBS, 2 August 1987.

82. Cleanth Brooks and Robert Penn Warren, *Understanding Fiction* (New York, 1943), 344–350.

83. Joseph Conrad, *Lord Jim* (New York, 1968), 130.

84. *Webster's New Collegiate Dictionary* (Springfield, Mass., 1973), 1253.

85. Norman Podhoretz, *Making It* (New York, 1967), 334.

86. Much of Milch's allure is based on his persona as the first and only Jewish amoralist; this dichotomy between moralizing Jews and manly men shows up in every TV show he's been associated with: *Hill Street Blues, Bay City Blues, Beverly Hills Buntz, Capital News*, and, currently, *NYPD Blue*, in which (the first year, anyway, before one of the leads left the show) the two Irish and Polish protagonist-cops didn't overworry the categorical imperative but at least are in touch with the elemental life force, while without exception every Jewish character—e.g., a lonely, whiny, conflicted lawyer named Goldstein or "4B," because that was his apartment number—was most emphatically not in touch with the elemental etc.

87. David Milch, "Two Chapters from 'The Groundlings,'" (MFA thesis, University of Iowa, 1970), 4, 7.

88. Ibid., 16, 19.

89. Ibid., 25–26.

90. From *The Poems of Stanley Kunitz, 1928–1978* (Boston, 1979), 50–51.

91. Gore Vidal, "Why I'm Not a Famous Novelist," *New York Times Book Review*, 30 August 1992, 26.

92. Richard Price, quoted in F. X. Feeney, "The Originator," *Movieline*, October 1992, 86.

93. Cynthia Ozick, quoted in "The Art of Fiction XCV," interview with Tom Teicholz, *Paris Review*, Spring 1987, 165.

94. John Updike, quoted in "The Art of Fiction XLIII," interview with Charles Thomas Samuels, *Paris Review*, Winter 1968, 89.

95. Arthur Schopenhauer, *The World as Will and Representation*, vol. 2, trans. E. F. J. Payne (New York, 1966), 508–509.

96. Letter from G. B. Edwards, Director of Audience Selection Staff, to the author, n.d.

97. Madonna, quoted on *Nightline*, ABC News, 3 December 1990.

98. Richard D. James, "Wall, S.D., Has Population of Only 800, but Its Drug Store Draws 10,000 a Day," *Wall Street Journal*, 5 September 1973, 12.

99. Dana Close Jennings, *Free Ice Water!* (Aberdeen, S.D., 1969), 6.

100. Ibid., 65.

101. Ibid., 63; Letter from Gayle Eisenbraun, Executive Secretary of Wall Drug, to the author, 16 September 1992: "We are not sure, but we think the shoplifting signs came down about three years ago. The management finally decided they were a bit much, and that considering we try to promote a relaxed atmosphere, they didn't fit in."

102. Postcards from the author to his parents, 30 June, 10 July, 4 July, 6 July, 7 July, 8 July, 9 July, 10 July 1965.

103. I was virtually certain that Pauline Kael—whom I've idolized since I was in junior high—had written this, but I couldn't find it anywhere, so I wrote her and asked if she could tell me where it was from. She called me and said it wasn't her line, but she liked it, and said she liked in general this ode to the movies, though she had a few minor criticisms, and then enumerated them over the next forty minutes.

104. Quotations from Rousseau's *Confessions*, 116–117.

105. "The Bunnies of Detroit," *Playboy*, August 1969, 139.

106. Roger Fanning, "Galapagos Islands, Guillotine Eyelids," *The Island Itself* (New York, 1991), 51.

107. Quoted in Inga Muscio, "Interview: Nina Hartley, Porcelain Blue Angel Eyes, Staring," *Stranger* 1, no. 20 (24 February 1992), 3.